THE MIDCENTURY MODERN LANDSCAPE

THE MIDCENTURY MODERN LANDSCAPE

ETHNE CLARKE

GIBBS SMITH
TO ENRICH AND INSPIRE HUMANKIND

"DESIGN IS THE CONSCIOUS EFFORT TO IMPOSE A MEANINGFUL ORDER"

VICTOR PAPANEK

TO LIVE IN A NEW WORLD

MAKE IT MIDCENTURY

Page 2: 'Aralia' textile design by Josef Frank for Svenskt Tenn, Sweden, c. 1928.

1

TO LIVE IN A NEW WORLD

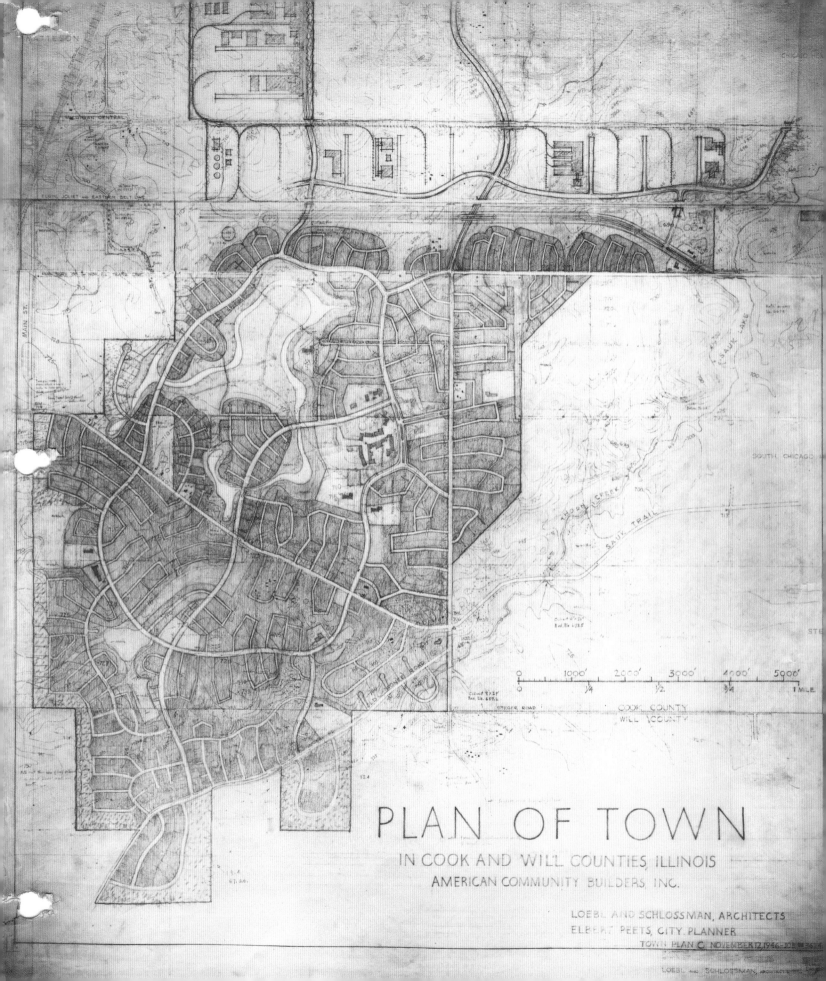

PLAN OF TOWN
IN COOK AND WILL COUNTIES, ILLINOIS
AMERICAN COMMUNITY BUILDERS, INC.

LOEBL AND SCHLOSSMAN, ARCHITECTS
ELBERT PEETS, CITY PLANNER
TOWN PLAN C NOVEMBER 12, 1946

LOEBL and SCHLOSSMAN, ARCHITECTS

Ours has been an age of great advances in science, medicine, and technology. Each day seems to bring a new promise of longer and healthier life spans, and devices that, we are assured, will make life more efficient. In the face of global pressures, faltering economies, war, dislocation, and uncommon cruelties that each day become more common and cruel, how many of us are on personal quests to dial back the stresses of daily life? We want to enrich our lives by living more simply, to bring our focus to the things that are core to our existence: family, home, and the spiritual well-being that comes from living a life in balance, more sustainably and less wastefully. More wisely.

This scenario would have been familiar sixty years ago. In the rebuilding after the Second World War, the focus was on family and the social promises brought by universal peace. Soldiers returned, married and restarted the careers they had put on hold (and became "road warriors" of the daily commute). Women were encouraged to give up their wartime factory jobs on the promise of a new, efficient, stress-free domesticity made possible by labor-saving appliances.

The economy was gathering steam. The emphasis was on creating new jobs and reigniting consumer spending. The building trades grew; entire new communities and dwellings, purposefully planned to accommodate young, middle-income professional families, were sprouting. Forward-looking design trends in architecture and the innovative use of building materials, which had been evolving post-First World War, but were repurposed to war

use as the Allied forces rearmed in the late 1930s, were returned to peacetime use: reinforced concrete, steel rebar, plate glass, plastics and synthetic fibers became more prevalent as the fabric of the new "modern" architecture expanded. Significantly, modest homes in planned suburbs boasted sweeps of lawn enriched by flower and shrub gardens. In mild climates, the swimming pool and patio were *de rigueur* components of the landscape. Electric lighting extended the day and electricity powered the new household appliances, which allowed more time for recreation, combined with open plan living and the blurring of exterior and interior spaces, shaped a new kind of lifestyle.

Park Forest, Illinois, where I was raised, was unique in being the first purpose-driven community developed in the 1940s and 1950s to accommodate returning military; young men, who, like my father, were recently graduated and about to launch careers when they were called up. The community was built on the site of a disused golf course. In a mix of town-house rental units and single-family dwellings, the streets wound through remnants of the landscaped golf course; wooded areas and grassland butted up against state-owned Forest Preserve land, where families would hike and cookout during the weekends.

The Park Forest master plan was such that schools and the shopping center (one of the first in the United States, with Park Forest's being modeled on the Piazza San Marco, Venice) were

INTRODUCTION

The master plan for the new suburb of Park Forest by Loebel, Schlossman and Bennett who made their name during the post-Second World War building boom. The town was described by the firm's former president, Don Hackl (FAIA), as a "prototypical suburb aimed at returning servicemen." But Park Forest wasn't just another subdivision project like Levittown, New York, but a complete community serving all needs: shopping, open space, schools and churches, and mixed housing.

Previous page: Emerging from the ashes of two World Wars, people found joy in new expressions of home and prosperity, as in the welcoming cheerfulness of midcentury modern design, like this Eichler home with its sunny atrium.

Overviews of Park Forest development: *above,* the shopping center was the hub of the community and the landmark Clock Tower at its center (demolished some years ago) was the fulcrum of civic events. Landscape architect Elbert Peets eschewed the grid so widely used in American settlements, preferring instead a landscape of sweeping curves, *right*, and "neighborhoods," as imagined in the sketch *opposite*, were key to the successful outcome of any planning effort.

Writing in 1948 to the editor of *The Journal of Housing*, Peets advised, "…the neighborhood—in some forms and degrees—is a very useful planning motif" because it caters for specific functions, "the first principle of modern urbanism." And by "simple logic" creates a service center with residential streets spreading from it, although not so far as to put it beyond reach.

within easy walking distance for wives and children. The men would use the family car for their daily commute, driving to the Illinois Central station where they would catch the train into Chicago. Spilling out onto Michigan Avenue, it was an easy walk for these white-collar workers to corporate headquarters of industry leaders like Shell Oil, advertising agencies and the like. It was an ordered universe in a world that once again was at peace.

What was it like to grow up in such a carefully planned, some might say controlled, environment? For children, surprisingly liberating. Each "court," as the blocks of town-house rentals were called, was ranged along a parking area onto which the kitchen and dining areas faced, while the front rooms looked onto common areas of mature trees and grass maintained by the grounds people of American Community Builders, who also looked after the fabric of the courts.

Sidewalks (ideal for tricycling, rollerskating and chalked games of hopscotch) circled the common space, with paths radiating off leading to each unit's front door; small lawns fronted each unit, too, and window boxes and flowerbeds were allowed so that each tenant had "land" to tend as they wished. There were no fences between the properties; the only ones I recall contained each court's small playground, so that little kids were corralled. The older kids had the freedom to race along the paths and run through the woods, only being called in from games of hide and seek when the lightning bugs began to flicker. The common area

was the court's gathering place for neighborly celebrations, cookouts and cocktail hour (another feature of the period).

Park Forest, as mentioned before, was built on the site of an old golf course community that had been planned for development in the 1920s, but never took off, going through several more failed iterations, including a proposal that it become a development marketed to African Americans.

In 1947, however, Philip M. Klutznick acquired the land along with some farmland that predated the golf course development, and proposed, at a press conference in Chicago's Palmer House, a self-governing community for 5,000 families, with a variety of housing types, to be located south of Chicago. His company, American Community Builders, advertised in the *Chicago Tribune,* which drew my parents to apply for tenancy; like all applicants, they were examined for veteran status, education and income. We were among the first families to arrive; by 1950, there were 3,000 residents living there, and few of the adults were over the age of thirty. Well-educated, burning with optimism to realize the potential of a bright new world, "starting from zero," my parents and their neighbors made the most of self-governing their village; ACB had almost from the beginning handed over the administration of Park Forest to a citizens' council, which oversaw the future planning and infrastructure of the village (which was also one of the first to use natural gas and to have all utility lines underground.)

Klutznick chose the prominent Chicago architectural firm Loebl, Schlossman & Bennett to develop Park Forest's master plan, design homes and churches, shopping centers and village amenities. The firm was innovative in developing a streamlined building method that meant construction was quick and smooth.

Looking at Park Forest's street plan, I recall the daily adventure of weaving through all the curving drives and undulating topography to reach my school, church and Girl Scouts meetings, and it's easy to understand what one of the firm's later partners meant when he described Richard Bennett's design approach: a lot of corners and angles to create curiosity; the "gee, what's around the next corner" human need to explore. In landscape planning this conceal/reveal is a way to increase the sense of space, because Park Forest was not an immense subdivision of a larger urban conglomeration like the Levittown, New York developments, but a small village, with a spacious core that made best use of existing topography (the undulating farm field remnants) and trees. One of my fondest memories is sitting under the apple blossoms garlanding an old tree in the middle of a still-in-use farm field behind my best friend's house, not far from the shopping center, Park Forest's urban core. To this day, the scent of apple blossom engenders feelings of happiness and security. For this memory I can thank the landscape architect for the project, Elbert Peets.

Born in Ohio in 1886, Peets was a graduate of Western Reserve University and in 1915 received a Master of Landscape Architecture from Harvard. He authored, in 1922, *The American Vitruvius: An Architect's Handbook of Civic Art,* a book that is still in reference today. He wrote a number of well-received articles, including "Restraint and Order in Planning Outdoor Rooms" (*Your Garden,*

1927) and "Site Planning for Livability" (*The American City,* 1941). For six years, until 1944, the U.S. Housing Authority employed Peets as Chief of the Site Planning Section. Then, from 1946—7, he joined forces with Klutznick, ACB and Richard Bennett as site planner for Park Forest, publishing in 1946 "Four Guides for Building a New Home" and in 1948, "The Neighborhood Concept," both for *The Journal of Housing.*

Peets evidently brought to the Park Forest city plan project the knowledge he had acquired on a year's journey (1920—1) through major European cities on a Charles Eliot Travelling Fellowship. Add to this the principles of greenbelt planning he evolved in the mid-1930s while working on planning and construction of Greendale, a new suburb of Milwaukee, Wisconsin.

Peets was particularly influenced by the redevelopment of Paris under Haussmann, who swept away the alleys and conduits of the medieval city and replaced them with broad and elegant avenues marked by classically inspired monuments at their termini symbolizing the power of the state and commerce, while graceful and well-manicured parks opening off shady tree-lined boulevards were a source of recreation and civility for city dwellers. In his later years, Peets undertook a reassessment of Pierre L'Enfant's master plan for the nation's capital. Washington D.C.'s stature as a humanistically inspired city had, he believed, been undermined by the indiscriminate siting of countless new monuments and memorial parks, streets that improved traffic flow but which disregarded people's need for recreation and neighborhoods. As a landscape master planner, Peets understood that the success of an urban center rests on meeting the needs of its inhabitants. There was, he and others at the time believed, a morality that

Left, a promotional flyer for the community of Greendale, built in 1935 following the Great Depression as part of the New Deal era. The development was intended to provide jobs and housing at reasonable rents, the landlord being the Federal Government. It was a greenbelt town, located on 3,400 acres of farmland south-east of Milwaukee. Elbert Peets was one of the lead site planners of a team that brought innovation to the development of the community; it was in this respect a precursor to Peets's work for Park Forest.

Opposite above, Peets's 1948 proposal for the continuing development of Greendale resembles his Park Forest plan for neighborhoods connected by service streets and pedestrian walkways feeding off throughways, each given its own landscape treatment. This is seen in his cross-section sketch, *opposite below left*, for recommended tree profiles for each type of street. *Opposite below right*, Peets's sketch for Park Forest's shopping plaza. The marketplace has long been seen as the hub of a community.

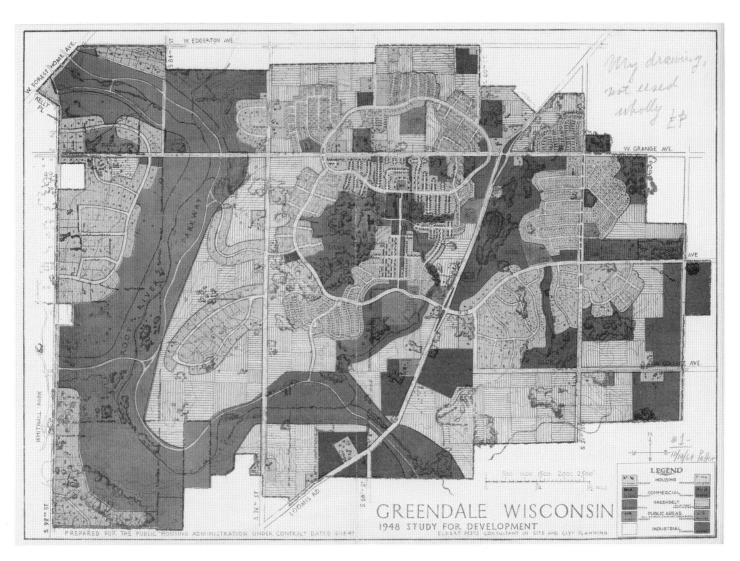

My drawing, not used wholly EP

GREENDALE WISCONSIN
1948 STUDY FOR DEVELOPMENT
PREPARED FOR THE PUBLIC HOUSING ADMINISTRATION UNDER CONTRACT DATED 6-14-47
ELBERT PEETS CONSULTANT IN SITE AND CITY PLANNING

LEGEND
HOUSING
COMMERCIAL
GREENBELT
PUBLIC AREAS
INDUSTRIAL

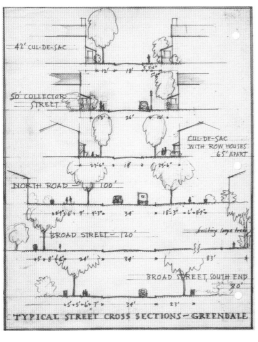

42' CUL-DE-SAC

50' COLLECTOR STREET

CUL-DE-SAC WITH ROW HOUSES 65' APART

NORTH ROAD — 100'

BROAD STREET — 120'

BROAD STREET SOUTH END — 80'

TYPICAL STREET CROSS SECTIONS — GREENDALE

SEARS

THE CENTURY OF PROGRESS

One of the early attempts at attracting investment in the development of Park Forest was made at the 1933 Chicago World's Fair. The promotion was not a success, but this particular World's Fair was, for it offered attendees the first glimmer of what modern living could be.

Known properly as the "Century of Progress," the Fair saw science and industry join hands to promote a vision of the future, one filled with ease and prosperity. In contrast to Chicago's 1893 fair, where white-clad, architectural classicism dominated (hence the popular name "The White City"), the Century of Progress was clad in the sharp angularities of Art Deco; the thirty-five buildings of the faux city were each accented from a palette of twenty-three vibrant colors, which also color coded each structure to help fairgoers find their way through tomorrow's world.

The fair blazed with nighttime illumination, too, and this lavish use of the incandescent bulb was the *sine qua non* of progress, and a symbol of all the Fair represented. In the words of the official guidebook:

"Science discovers, genius invents, industry applies, and man adapts himself to, or is molded by, new things... A Century of Progress undertakes to clothe science with its true garb of practical reality and to tell its story of humanly significant achievement [...] And the story is made complete, its sequence a running narrative, by the exhibits of social science, which shows you how Man has come up from the caves of half a hundred thousand years ago [...] responding to each new thing discovered and developed. You see man's march upward to the present day, where, in a home of 1933, he uses and enjoys all the multitudinous benefits with which science and industry have endowed him."

A fair amount of hyperbolic optimism, maybe, but remember, in 1933 the world had found its way back from the First World War and the annihilation of nearly an entire generation of young men.

As luck would have it, the 1933 World's Fair opened just as the Great Depression was hitting bottom; soon the New Deal would ignite a return to some kind of prosperity, but then came the Second World War. It took another fifteen years, but the idea of The Century of Progress had not died, and it wasn't long before the engines of industry were turning again, and prosperity and people began to believe that happiness was just around the corner.

The 1933 Chicago World's Fair marked a midpoint between two World Wars that shaped the twentieth century.

must underpin the development of new communities, and which impacted everything from the way the houses were designed and deployed to the way the streets intersected and pavements for foot traffic wove through the fabric of the place. And there was, in almost all cases, a desire on the part of many landscape architects, to reflect and respect the *genius loci.*

Inevitably, there were numerous practitioners, but they have been largely overshadowed by ones whose talents for design, and in some cases self-promotion, gave them lasting recognition. Investigating the midcentury modern period has introduced me to some of these shadow figures. It has also reinforced my understanding of the great design continuum, and amused me to see how history repeats itself as each generation of landscape designers, architects and horticulturists kicked against its antecedents' aesthetics to arrive at their own design parti.

Thus, Elbert Peets disliked Olmsted, writing that Central Park, Olmsted's most recognized work, divided the landscape from the city, and because of that was unnatural. Jens Jensen complained that Peets's work did not honor the native landscape because he used too many exotic trees and thus Peets's landscapes were uncomfortable and unsympathetic, not speaking to the soul of place or person.

In gratitude

For their advice, guidance and valuable insights into the driving influences of the midcentury modern period, I especially thank Dwight S. Brothers, former Professor of Economics, Harvard University, and architectural historian Elaine Freed, former executive director of the Frank Lloyd Wright Home and Studio, Oak Park, Illinois and a past vice president of the Frank Lloyd Wright Foundation, Scottsdale, Arizona. She has advised on my research, shared her insights and library most generously, and her 2003 book, *Modern at Mid-century: the Early Fifties Houses of Ingraham and Ingraham,* introduced me to the work of Frank Lloyd Wright's granddaughter, Elizabeth Ingraham, in Colorado Springs. Many of Ingraham's houses are around the corner from my own small midcentury modern ranch, with its echoes of Cliff May and a blank slate for a garden. It has been a journey to bring it back from the embossed wall-papered, net-curtained, and cabin-in-the-woods, 1980s look to the spare but undeniably comfortable, 1950s open plan with the garden and patio just a step away through the sliding glass doors. Elaine Freed's recent book, *Modern at Mid-century: Ruhtenberg Revisited* (Rhyolite Press, 2017) adds to our knowledge of the period by examining how architect Jan Ruhtenberg's work in Germany, Sweden, and America salutes his famous mentor, Mies van der Rohe.

Long relationships have been the bedrock on which this book was built: Anna Mumford, founder of Filbert Press, Bath, England and the UK publisher, Frances Lincoln, have been wonderful creative partners for many years, and continue to be so. I am so grateful to Anna and the FL team for asking me to write this book and for their support throughout the process. In this I was lucky to have Anna Watson as my editor; she kept a steady hand on the wheel, steering through our email tsumanis, all the while hunting down archive images and working with architects and landscape designers around the world to source the wonderful images that fill this book.

Through it all, my husband Donald has been my de facto copy editor, sounding board and lead cheerleader, along with our "kids," David and his wife, our much-loved daughter-in-law, Saream Tuong Clarke. Couldn't, wouldn't, do this without y'all.

Ethne Reuss Clarke
Colorado Springs, Colorado, Winter 2016

"The Landscape Priesthood," an article by Elbert Peets published in the January 1927 issue of *The American Mercury*, lobbed a bomb into the hallowed halls of the American Society of Landscape Architecture. Peets declared, "American landscape architecture is now a huge joke. It has produced a few pleasant reproductions of Surrey landscape and a few charming Italian gardens. But as a vital, evolving art it is dead." He went on to lambast the "revered Olmsted" for his Anglophilia, devotion to English art critic John Ruskin and to the English landscape, especially the carefully composed parks of England's great estates.

Not a man to mince his words, Peets decried the devotion of American landscape architects and their (wealthy) clients to "the English landscape style [...] a calamity of the first magnitude." He ridiculed Central Park as being far from the antidote to New York's slums, since the only people to benefit were not the Irish who had to walk three miles from their tenement slums to get there, but the "carriage-owning Protestants of English ancestry." Peets carried on in this vein, targeting the American Society of Landscape Architects for being elitist and out of touch with the true needs of the craft, remarking that, "Italy was not made beautiful by artists so much as by peasants and laborers," who preferred the symmetrically organized "folk art" garden, because, as Peets condescendingly asserted, formal, linear and balanced arrangements in design were all that could be understood by the "simple minds who do the great mass of building and gardening."

The landscape style defined by carefully sited groves of trees, shaped by undulating masses of shrubbery and streams coaxed into visually pleasing curves criss-crossed by pretzel-shaped paths winding through and around and across the whole, was unnatural and the antithesis of the "folk language" that could define a truly American landscape. Only trained professionals could execute "natural" landscape design, an idea promoted by the practitioners of the art: "...under this foliage of logical distinction," Peets asserted, "will be found the fungi of economic interest."

Emergence of the "Prairie School"

This was not a new debate. The same tune had been playing in England for fifty years before it crossed to the American market. The attributes of formal vs. informal and "wild" vs. landscaped, gardeners vs. architects, had in the late nineteenth to early twentieth centuries stimulated heated arguments between, most notably, the plantsman and "Father of the English Flower Garden," William Robinson (who favored natural landscape created by gardeners) and Arts and Crafts architects, Reginald Blomfield and John Dando Sedding (who preferred formal design, with particular emphasis on the English late medieval/early Renaissance periods, as fashioned by architects).

In the United States, digging back two decades before Peets laid his professional neck on the line, a Virginian named Wilhelm

FRANK LLOYD WRIGHT AND FINDING A LANGUAGE FOR MODERN ARCHITECTURE AND LANDSCAPE

Wright's home in rural Wisconsin, Taliesin, keeps a low profile—the better to merge with surrounding pastureland.

Miller picked up his pen and began to write for a new magazine, *Country Life in America,* that was edited by his former professor at Cornell, the renowned botanist and horticulturist Liberty Hyde Bailey. Miller's agenda promoted an American style of landscape design, and he urged his readers to forsake the *gardenesque*, described by him as a "miscellaneous and meaningless collection of curiosities" (i.e., exotic plants) derived, he believed, from English models.

The better to refine his argument with first-hand knowledge, Miller travelled to England in 1908, after which he concluded that the desirable course for American gardeners was to use plants native to the locale, as they were the ones that were best suited to the site and would therefore give a purely authentic and distinctive American identity. A series of articles on this not-entirely-original proposal was in 1911 made into the book *What England Can Teach Us About Gardening.* (Curiously, Miller, in seeking out what could be learned from the English garden to inform the creation of a uniquely American vocabulary of design, was transmitting William Robinson's ideal of the "wild garden." That he had visited Robinson at Gravetye Manor in 1908, while traveling in England, may have helped him form his ideas.)

The purpose of the book, he set out immediately, was to "inspire people to make more and better gardens," by emphasizing the regional character of one's landscape that would help them to achieve that goal. "In every part of America we should study

nature and make garden pictures full of local color." Those last two words became his descriptor for American style, at least until Miller met Jens Jensen and saw in his work the exact expression of what he was championing. In 1914, he published an article titled "The New Prairie School," followed in 1915 by a book, *The Prairie Spirit in Landscape Gardening.* It was not long before the term "Prairie School" became, and remained, the synonym for American design in landscape, and to some degree American architecture, particularly as expressed in the work of Frank Lloyd Wright, even though the great man disavowed any connection to the movement.

At the time of the 1933 Century of Progress World's Fair, America's greatest living architect was Frank Lloyd Wright. Nearing seventy years old, he had been practicing since the late nineteenth century, and had evolved a distinct vocabulary for twentieth-century American architecture, designing extraordinary houses for wealthy social elites as well as a number of impressive public buildings.

Wright was a midwesterner, and the prairie landscape was his lexicon. In his designs, the unbroken prairie horizon spread beneath a brilliant, sun-filled sky was translated into deep overhanging eaves supported by walls paneled with large windows that mirrored the vastness of the heavens.

By contrast, the interior of a Wright building was at first cave-like, with low-ceilings and dark walls, but once into the main rooms the ceiling soared and natural light flooded the space. Before

FOR MR GEORGE BERDAN   FRANK LLOYD WRIGHT   ARCHITECT

Wright, windows existed, seemingly, to support swathes of blinds and curtains, and to exclude the outdoors; now they brought it in. As Wright wrote in his book *The Natural House* (Horizon Press, 1954), "You may see that walls are vanishing," and humans, he described, were finally moving out of the cave.

In 1937, Wright designed the first of his "Usonian" houses; modest affordable homes for middle-income families, hitching his wagon to the move toward building communities for the "working man." The main difference between Wright's buildings and the houses built in the Levittown, New York subdivision after 1947, for example, was that the latter were produced to a standardized layout with one completed every fifteen minutes, while the Usonian homes were individually designed to reflect the needs of the client and the site. Each Usonian home took several months to complete, and though reasonably priced relative to a Wright Prairie home, were affordable only to the better-off section of the middle class: they were not for the masses.

In the *Natural Home,* Wright set out his defining principles for domestic design, which amounted to a list of dos and don'ts. Among the dos were flat or slant roofs, carports (rather than garages), brick, wood and glass interiors, overhanging eaves, and the use wherever possible, of "natural" materials. In the absence of any evidence that Wright actively designed landscapes or gardens to complement his buildings, it is possible to infer from

BEFORE WRIGHT, WINDOWS EXISTED, SEEMINGLY, TO SUPPORT SWATHES OF BLINDS AND CURTAINS, AND TO EXCLUDE THE OUTDOORS; NOW THEY BROUGHT IT IN

Wright believed every American had the right to own a home: Usonian was a semaphore for US Own. The houses were technologically advanced and built of low-maintenance materials, but didn't compete with tract housing programs that could be put up in days. Each Usonian home was bespoke to fit the client's needs and the building site, often taking months to complete.

his "do" list that if he had, the gardens would have been early precursors of today's popular "prairie" style: broad sweeps of native grasses enriched by native perennials, a carefully positioned tree chosen for its characterful form and the quality of its shadow play. As can be seen today in his best-known structures, Fallingwater in Pennsylvania and his own homes, Taliesin in Wisconsin and Taliesin West in Arizona, Wright built into and with the landscape, recognizing in layout and materials the *genius loci*.

Though on the evidence of their correspondence it might seem unlikely, Wright's championing of native plants may well have been inspired by his association with Jens Jensen: by drawing on the natural features of his native Midwest, in particular the broad horizontals of the wide open spaces, Wright led the movement toward creating a lasting legacy of American architecture. Jensen, meanwhile, was his horticultural counterpart, finding in the landscape of the midwestern prairies the compositional beauty and natural harmony he found lacking in other environments.

The civilizing power of nature

Emigrating from Denmark, Jensen arrived in the US in 1884, aged 24. He found his way to Chicago, and before long, enamored by the prairie biome and filled with a convert's passion, he was creating the city parks that have become his lasting legacy—Humboldt, Garfield, and Douglas—along with a host of smaller green spaces.

The Forest Preserve system in Cook County, Illinois, owes its existence to Jensen's early work establishing a strong conservation lobby in Illinois. His core belief was that for their wellbeing people needed to be in daily contact with nature, by which he meant native plants and their habitats. His was, it has been said, "a near-mystical belief" in the healing and civilizing power of nature. Jensen drew heavily on the vernacular, using native stone to construct "council rings."

These stone-encircled firepits became his signature—one was included in nearly every one of his plans, although clients often asked for them to be removed since they were little used. But his understanding of and reverence for native plants was a clear statement of his dislike for European models of classical landscape. He and Wright had a distant but respectful relationship for nearly thirty-five years, collaborating on only five projects across twenty-eight years. Their correspondence reveals Wright's sense of frustration at the many personal setbacks he had experienced and his affront at being ignored while newer faces claimed the limelight. Writing to Jensen in 1930 that "even friends (like yourself for instance) seldom give a hand unless dragged in by the beard," Wright mused that in twenty-seven years neither had put any work in the way of the other, and wondered if that was "because a Star is seldom willing to share with a Star?" A remark that Jensen rebuffed, advising Wright to be thankful for what he had, and not to dwell on what he had missed out on.

HIS WAS, IT HAS BEEN SAID, "A NEAR MYSTICAL BELIEF" IN THE HEALING AND CIVILIZING POWER OF NATURE

Tirranna, or the Rayward-Shepherd house, was designed by Wright in 1955 for a pond-side site in New Canaan, Connecticut. The living areas overlook extensive water gardens and rock work designed by Frank Okamura, the landscape architect for Brooklyn Botanic Gardens.

Previous page: Taliesen West, on the desert outside Scottsdale, Arizona was developed from 1937 as Wright's winter home and desert outpost for his school of architecture. Wright drew heavily on the long low contours of the native landscape in the design and local rock in its construction. He remarked that "Arizona needs its own architecture."

Jens Jensen, a landscape architect and colleague of Frank Lloyd Wright, shared the latter's respect for native materials and the wild places of the American Midwest. But in his case, Jensen honored the plants and landforms of the places he touched. Humboldt Park in Chicago, *above,* was one such project, and in his rehabilitation of the original park and its waterways, Jensen created a seemingly natural landscape. Reconsidering the plan for the landscape, Jensen, *left,* also included a formal garden, *opposite above*, bringing together landscape elements that he recognized would enrich the lives of city dwellers who had, "no other gardens except their windowsills." Council rings, *opposite below,* were a signature Jensen feature, representing community while honoring the Native American traditions of communal discourse and collaboration.

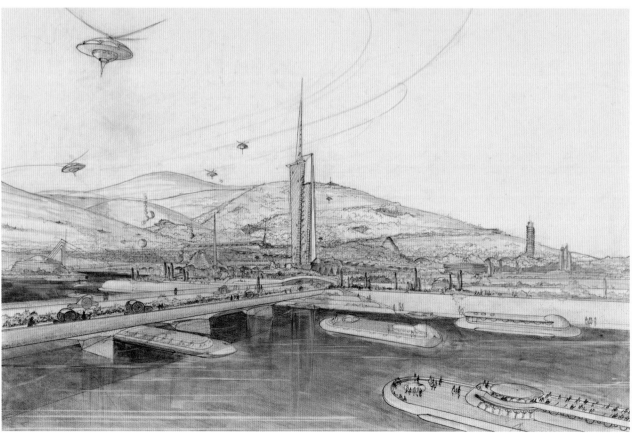

Both men created schools: Wright's Taliesin was introduced in 1932, following a lengthy period of money and personal problems; Jensen's The Clearing was launched in 1935. Dubbed the "school of the soil," it was an idea that Jensen had nurtured for some time—at least from his earliest days founding and working with conservation groups such as the Prairie Club, a society for nature enthusiasts, and later Friends of Our Native Landscape, targeting those who had some influence in the conservation realm. But the idea for creating a school that focused on nature study and conservation only came into its own with the death of his much-loved wife Anne Marie, and an energizing visit to Taliesin West in 1934.

Commissions from Wright's wealthy clients paid the bills, but he was ever a champion of better housing for the working man, and it was Wright's petition for support of his planned community Broadacre City that finally frayed the thin bond of friendship between the two men: Jensen refused to sign, allegedly writing "Go to Hell" across the envelope before returning it unopened to Wright. He later wrote to him saying that his own close association to the soil meant he understood better than Wright what humanity's true purpose was on the earth. Wright responded by insulting Jensen, calling him a "realistic landscapist" who delighted in creating "superficial exterior effects" by "using nature's objects to make your effects."

And what, we could ask, is wrong with that? One of Jensen's biggest commissions was for Henry Ford's estate at Fair Lane in Dearborn, Michigan. At the heart of the plan was a long meadow that reached toward the horizon in the direction of the setting sun, which could be viewed comfortably from the house terrace, or approached by a gentle meander through the tree-hemmed meadow. Plantings were seasonal, the view constant but changing as deciduous shrubs and trees changed guise through the year. Mrs. Ford, however, wanted her rose gardens and perennial borders, which Jensen arrayed in orderly geometric beds close to the house. But in designing as he did, it is as though he was always aware that one day the garden might be abandoned. In his book, *Siftings,* he explained his core belief that the garden was an ephemeral, artificial creation. "Let the garden disappear in the bosom of nature of which it is a part, and though the hand of man is not visible, his spirit remains as long as the plants he planted grow and scatter their seed."

Jensen called on nature for inspiration in all that he did, putting his energy into landscape preservation and nature conservation—gardens would not be missed, but nature must endure. Always, Jensen aimed to "keep the hand of man" out of the frame, but looked for ways to entice humanity into an enjoyment and appreciation of natural landscape.

"LET THE GARDEN DISAPPEAR IN THE BOSOM OF NATURE OF WHICH IT IS A PART, AND THOUGH THE HAND OF MAN IS NOT VISIBLE, HIS SPIRIT REMAINS AS LONG AS THE PLANTS HE PLANTED GROW AND SCATTER THEIR SEED"

From 1932 until his death in 1959, Wright gestated a plan for a new kind of urban center, which he named Broadacre City, shown in his sketches *opposite*. In common with other architects of his stature (and not to be outdone), Wright was proposing a socio-political statement in urban planning. In doing so, he moved from designing tightly controlled environments for private clients to imposing rigidly defined habitats for entire communities across the United States that would be shaped by automobile travel and other more futuristic transport systems.

NORTH WEST ELEVATION. ¼" Scale.

SOUTH WEST ELEVATION. ¼" Scale.

NORTH EAST ELEVATION. Scale ¼" = 1 foot.

SOUTH EAST ELEVATION. Scale ¼" = 1 foot.

SKETCH ELEVATION FOR A
SMALL COTTAGE FOR
MR. W. J. BAILEY
LA JOLLA CALIF.

Irving J. Gill
Architect
Carlsbad Calif.

Tel. 510 J.
Box 595
Jan. 27th 1932.

"We are doomed for the rest of our generation to live with boxhouses and pre-fabs within sight everywhere... It doesn't seem possible with modern building methods that have to be used for economic reasons to devise anything that looks decent," wrote the English architect Cecil Pinsent in 1947. His observation was directed to his first client, the art connoisseur Bernard Berenson, for whom he had created the elegant Villa I Tatti and its extensive formal gardens in Tuscany. I Tatti was an essay in Renaissance ideals of architecture blended with a modern sensibility about the modeling of space.

While Berenson had remained in Florence, Italy, during the war, Pinsent left the city in 1938 and returned to England. Florence had been his home since 1907 and the majority of his work had been executed there, but having toughed it out in Italy during the First World War, with the onset of the Second World War he felt compelled to leave. Recognizing that war would considerably reduce the work available from wealthy clients, he was unable to accept the Fascist regime's requirement that all architects be registered as engineers. For him, and for others like him, the art of architecture and landscape could not be separated from the craftsmanship required of each. Not a surprising stance for an architect schooled in the Arts and Crafts tradition of late nineteenth-century England at a time when the formal classicism and ornamentation of the high Victorian period was yielding to the stripped-down modernism to come.

Pinsent was one of a number of young architects whose work bridged that gap between Beaux Arts classicism and unadorned modernism in the early years of the twentieth century. In the United States, Irving Gill opened his San Diego office in 1907 and began turning out refined homes built for practical living; carrying little ornament they were flat-roofed and whitewashed, sitting uneventfully in their plots making no particular demands on the landscape. In Vienna, Adolf Loos designed with reverence for classical geometry, *sans* ornamentation. Another was English architect John Archibald Campbell, who, like Pinsent, established his reputation in Europe, in his case in Germany, arriving there in 1902. Both brought a refined simplicity to their designs, Pinsent comprehending the essence of Renaissance form, Campbell ignoring the then popular *Jugendstil* (German Art Nouveau) sensuality in favor of his own brand of clean, rational design. And though at the forefront of a shift toward the modern, all shared an appreciation of the landscape traditions that preceded them and a common respect for Arts and Crafts, while seeking a way to express functional design without sacrificing the humanism of architecture.

La Foce, created by Cecil Pinsent for Iris and Antonio Origo, was a remodel of an old coaching inn on the Siena to Florence road. Pinsent expanded the existing interior spaces, opening them onto courtyard gardens that framed views of the spartan landscape of the Val d'Orcia. His work there was not confined to the villa, as he collaborated with the Origos to build a school, a hospital and modern housing for the estate workers' families; Antonio Origo was determined to drag Italy's medieval farming system into the

BAUHAUS BOWS OUT

Early modernism in the United States emerged in the work of architects like Irving Gill, whose design for the Wheeler J. Bailey house, *opposite,* built in La Jolla, California and dating from 1907, shows traces of the Arts and Crafts tendency to vernacular decoration, as in the roof overhang, bay window articulations, and suggestion of plants cladding the walls and foundations. The drawing also hints at the emergence of the spare "cubist" lines of the International Style.

twentieth century, uplifting the workers whose families had been tied to the land for generations, but had little to show for it. Pinsent returned to La Foce after the Second World War to execute a few final projects before his death in 1947.

Birchens Spring (later renamed Drummer's Yard) is one of John Archibald Campbell's best-known buildings. Writing in *Country Life* in 1938, Christopher Hussey observed that in plan the house was like a series of pavilions, and the garden terrace a reinterpretation of the modernist model for outdoor living as a "big summer-time extension of the house." He later described it in Nikolaus Pevsner's *Buckinghamshire*: "The echoes are of the English manor house and Futurist paintings of De Chirico."

Campbell's work was not confined to manor houses, either. He drew up plans for apartment buildings to house bombed-out Londoners. As he wrote, "I believe that I can take the poor man's home and make it what it should be: honest and true and worthy of a man to live in it. I intend to try and break through the monstrous convention that 'architecture' is for the rich and jerry-building is for the rest. For if architecture is not for all, it is for none."

The First World War had made all that difficult and at its end, in France alone, it was estimated that 6,147 public buildings had to be demolished, 293,039 homes were completely destroyed and nearly 500,000 severely damaged. The 1918 Armistice signaled not only a demand for rapid and well-organized reconstruction, but also fostered a highly charged political agenda; the devastation of that

John Archibald Campbell and Cecil Pinsent were English architects who moved to Europe in the early 1900s; the former practiced mostly in Germany, and the latter in Tuscany. Both bridged the gap between English Arts and Crafts and European Modernism, and just as their American contemporary Irving Gill did, submerged any tendency to applied decoration in a reverence for unsullied lines and clean curves. The arcade and courtyard at Campbell's

Birchens Spring in England, *above right*, has an introspective austerity, echoing Italian painter Giorgio De Chirico's series *Melanconia* (1912-16), *above left*. While at I Tatti, Settignano, *opposite above*, and La Foce, Chianciano Terme, *opposite below*, Pinsent borrowed late Renaissance architectural forms and motifs and translated them into a clean but beguiling use of space and ornament

calamitous war changed the socio-economic status of Europe in ways that America never experienced.

Machines for living

Answering this need led to the development of the Bauhaus, a German arts and crafts school begun by Walter Gropius in 1919, and founded in the atmosphere of artistic and intellectual freedom that characterized the Weimer Republic after the First World War.

Bauhaus shared many of its ideals with the English Arts and Crafts movement; fundamental to its credo was the idea that all art was one art—that one could not differentiate between what was "art" and what was "craft"—and that the uniqueness of artistic output could be as equally expressed in mass- or industrial-scale production as in hand-crafted, individually designed works. The industrialization of architecture, if it can be called that, and need for efficiency in reconstruction was met by the widespread adoption of Taylorism, developed in the 1880s by an American engineer, Frederick Winslow Taylor. Also known as Scientific Management, it proposed to organize labor around a system of quasi-scientific manufacturing efficiencies and increase productivity via wage incentives.

One of the earliest adapters of Taylorism was a French architect, Charles-Édouard Jeanneret, later known as Le Corbusier, or Corbu. In his book *Aprés le Cubisme* published 18 November 1918, he stated, "The war has ended: all is organized; all is clear and purified; factories are built; nothing is just like it was before the War; …it destroyed

senile methods and replaced with those which the battle proved best." And continued, "Taylorism is not a question of anything more than exploiting intelligently scientific discoveries [and] principles of analysis, organization and classification." For Le Corbusier believed, as other architects before him had, that architects were also social engineers, and architecture, practiced along Tayloristic lines, the tool with which they produced low-cost, mass housing. And in his terms, a house was "a machine for living." Such houses could be built on a production line inspired by Henry Ford's Model T: Fordism held hands with Taylorism in the evolution of mechanistic architecture, which came to be called the International Style.

In postwar Germany, Gropius and the Bauhaus school embraced Taylorism, merging the practicalities of factory production with the aesthetic ideals of Arts and Crafts creation, preserving the authenticity of the latter with the efficiencies of the former. Gropius believed that architecture and design were particularly suited to this approach. Furthermore, the Bauhausian articles of faith began with "Truth to Materials," i.e., construction methods should be evident and their nature not disguised, and that the pursuit of honesty and simplicity in their art should guide all designers/craftspeople. Teachers at the Bauhaus school included Le Corbusier, Mies van der Rohe, Eileen Gray, Marcel Breuer and Florence Bassett Knoll. Machines for living gave birth to mass-produced, steel tube-framed furniture, built-in units that streamlined interiors, textiles that incorporated new synthetics, dyes and weaving techniques, and

The Masters' House at Dessau, *opposite*, part of the Bauhaus complex, was established by Walter Gropius as a center for interdisciplinary studies in design. There was no department of architecture, yet Gropius taught that architecture was everywhere, and that the architect was responsible for all aspects of the designed world. At Bauhaus, the Arts and Crafts aesthetic of the handmade was applied to the machine-made, and Bauhaus buildings resembled factories. It was the age of the machine—and the combustion engine—and in France, Le Corbusier grafted the efficiencies of the automobile production line into his architectural output, as at the Villa Stein in Garches, France, *right*.

Villa Savoye, located on the urban fringe of Paris and completed in 1939, was the last of Le Corbusier's "white villas," a series of private houses built in what became known as the International Style. Made of concrete, it utilizes all of the elements central to Le Corbusier's design theory—his five points of architecture: a flat roof for recreation, strips of bypass windows bisecting the exterior, open plan interiors, an unelaborated façade, and pillars supporting the main structure so

that, in this instance, it floats above an unsullied meadow. Apparently, Le Corbusier intended a small herd of cattle to be pastured on the property; they would be able to roam unhindered beneath and around the house—a touch of pastoral naturalism to offset the extra-terrestrial structure.

tableware that looked like exercises in geometry. They became the Bauhaus signature, gracing the interiors of many midcentury homes.

What was the response of these brave new designers and theoreticians to nature, to landscape, or to the idea of the "garden" (a concept that Le Corbusier and others no doubt regarded old hat)? In comparison to Frank Lloyd Wright's homes, which were decidedly not machines for living, and that blended sympathetically, if almost seamlessly, into their native surrounding, the structures of the International Style sat in their landscape like spaceships that had just landed. Perhaps this was because there was no way to mechanize nature? Le Corbusier imagined his houses as white boxes on stilts, stalking through meadows where cattle roamed free around and below the buildings—like ground-floor cattle stalls beneath European peasant farmhouses, *sans* walls.

Other architects espoused the health-giving properties of wide-open windows. Many simply fell back on the idea of the eighteenth-century English landscape park of rolling lawns and clumps of gracefully pruned trees, but this was frowned upon as being a mere romanticized representation of nature, not scientific in its approach to utilizing nature in support of architectural reason. Horticultural education was not part of an architect's training; there were, however, plantsmen and women at work trying to systematize and tabulate the cultivation of shrubs, perennials and exotic ornamentals.

At the turn of the twentieth century, the German plant breeder, Willy Lange, was postulating that landscape should be shaped in the contours of the motherland; the nation's ancient pine forests, wooded hills and heather-carpeted moors were his inspiration. Observing nature and the associations formed within it served as the basis for Lange's naturalistic designs. He wrote that it was essential to provide conditions appropriate for a plant's physical needs as well as for the needs of its "soul" and preferred associations, not to imitate nature in our gardens but to be guided by it: "A garden will be a work of art if we enrich nature within the limitations of natural processes." In time, Lange's direction expanded to allow the introduction of "foreign" plants, but only if their cultural requirements were compatible with those of their native companions in the garden. A decade before the rise of the Third Reich, Lange's approach was regarded as in line with the rising fever of nationalism and racism of the times.

Karl Foerster was Lange's contemporary, and every bit as observant of nature's processes and passionate about plants, which led him to investigate the ornamental uses of ferns and grasses (for which modern gardeners owe him profound thanks). Foerster, while appreciating native plants and the importance of understanding their shared cultural needs, also favored a more architectural approach to design; he much admired English formal gardens, perennial borders and a well-framed garden picture. The architect Hermann Muthesius and his book *Das Englishche Haus*, published in 1904, may well have fostered his appreciation. Sponsored by the German government, Muthesius produced a lexicon of what made his subject so livable, and to a large extent credited the English garden, of which he wrote:

Calamagrostis x acutiflora 'Karl Foerster', commonly known as Foerster's feather reed grass, has become a fixture in contemporary gardens. Hardy and adaptable to a variety of growing conditions, it is just one of Foerster's many selections that has brought structure to "natural" gardens via plants as opposed to plans.

"The garden is seen as a continuation of the rooms of the house, almost a series of separate outdoor rooms, each of which is self-contained and performs a separate function. Thus the garden *extends* [author's italics] the house into the midst of nature. At the same time it gives it a framework in nature, without which it would stand like a stranger in its surroundings. In aesthetic terms the ordered garden is to the house as the socle to the statue, the base on which it stands."

And so, between the World Wars, the sturdy perennial debate between wild/natural gardens and formal/architectural gardens rolled on, with Foerster attracting a greater following among the next generation of landscape designers and architects. Foerster did not share Lange's nationalistic interpretation of nature, and resisted Nazi demands that his nursery sell only "pure" German native plants.

The year 1933 may have seen the Century of Progress in Chicago, but in 1937 in Munich, the Nazi Party staged *Entartete Kunst,* the Degenerate Art exhibition, a roundup of Expressionist painting and sculpture denounced by Hitler as work that went against German sensibilities and nature. Into the rapidly widening cultural abyss fell the Bauhaus school and its various northern European satellites, and their adherents—many of whom were Jewish and already targeted—were identified as communist-influenced and guilty of promoting "degenerate art." The exodus

The Gropius House, *below* and *opposite*, was the family home that he designed after arriving in the United States to teach at Harvard. He and his wife decided that the vernacular architecture of New England did not suit their style, so they built this Bauhausian house. The surrounding landscape—always a prime consideration for Gropius—was another matter, and he integrated stacked stone walls, native trees and boulder-studded grassy meadows into the home's design and construction.

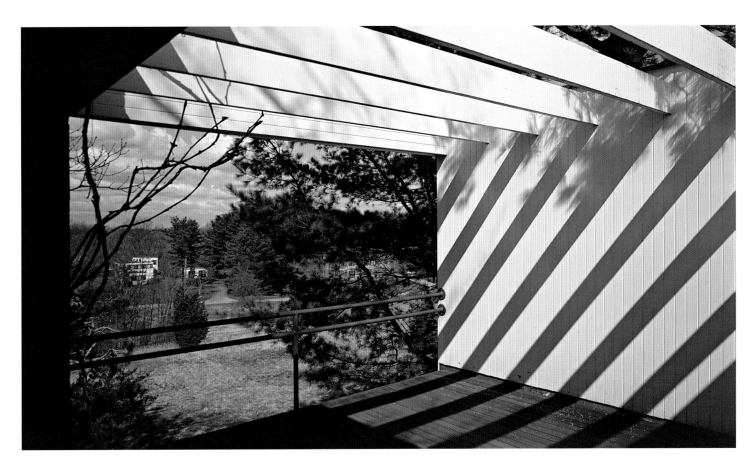

"THE GARDEN IS SEEN AS A CONTINUATION OF THE ROOMS OF THE HOUSE, ALMOST A SERIES OF SEPARATE OUTDOOR ROOMS, EACH OF WHICH IS SELF-CONTAINED AND PERFORMS A SEPARATE FUNCTION"

Pages 40-41: Architect Philip Johnson's contribution to the New Canaan, Connecticut, scene was the Glass House, built in 1949. Its complete transparency ensured a seamless merging with the surrounding landscape, which in concert with the interior layout, ushered in the concept of open plan living. Johnson drew his inspiration for the house from the site—a grassy knoll and an oak tree— describing the aspect as more of an English landscape park than a garden of flowers.

of creative talent was underway, and by the mid 1930s, Bauhaus teachers and students, artists, musicians, writers, composers— anyone espousing the heretical creed of modernism—were beginning to impact the arts in Israel and the Americas and other countries to which they fled. However degenerate the Bauhaus may have been cast by the Nazi regime, this did not prevent Fascist architects from adopting elements of the International Style because of its apparent functionalism; but they transformed it into an overbearing hash of geometric forms soused in a thin gruel of classical triumphalism.

Gropius and Breuer went first to London, and later both men went to the United States to teach at the Harvard Graduate School of Design. Breuer had been one of the first students Gropius admitted to the Bauhaus and throughout his life Gropius remained Breuer's mentor and sometime architectural partner.

Even though the sophisticates of the East Coast art scene received the arrival of the Europeans with some excitement, the transplanting did not go easily and was not exactly an overnight sensation. Harvard's school of architecture dropped the decorative formalism of Beaux Arts and embraced the International Style-inspired functionalism. Frank Lloyd Wright's vision for a wholly American language of architecture and landscape inspired by the colors and textures of the rolling Midwestern plains was sidelined in favor of white boxes and flat roofs. The only American art form that survived being usurped by the incomers was jazz.

ELIOT NOYES AND NEW CANAAN MODERNISTS

Eliot Noyes was a consummate industrial designer and also a visionary architect of the mid-century modern period. It could be said that Noyes designed his houses by climate zone—he believed that climate was the point of departure for good building and that climate thus gave each region its own style, supported by simple forms and the undisguised use of materials.

Born in Boston, Massachusetts, Noyes received his degree in architecture from Harvard Graduate School of Design in 1938. There he met and was influenced by Le Corbusier, was taught by Gropius and Breuer, and briefly joined their practice in Cambridge, Massachusetts before becoming the director of industrial design at the Museum of Modern Art in New York. Noyes was at MoMA until 1946, taking leave during the Second World War to serve as an advisor to the United States Air Force.

In 1947, Noyes built the first of the two houses he designed for his family in New Canaan, Connecticut. He'd settled there and then attracted Breuer, Phillip Johnson and two other Harvard alumni to the area; they became known as the Harvard Five, and put the small town on the map as the nexus of East Coast modernist architecture. Of the 100 or so homes built in New Canaan from the late 1940s through the 1950s, a number are listed on the US National Register of Historic Places, including that icon of picture-window American modernism, Phillip Johnson's Glass House, and the second Noyes family home built in 1954 (the first is not extant).

In 1969, in an article for *Art in America* magazine, Noyes wrote about his new idea for the design of houses.

"It started, I think, with my own house in New Canaan, Connecticut. This is really two houses flanking a court and held together by two massive stone walls, each ninety-nine feet long and a foot and half thick. Except for one large entrance with barn doors in the center of each wall, these walls have no openings, and their stone surfaces show on both sides, inside the house and out. To a large extent they set the character of the house."

The walls also are evidence of Noyes's appreciation for local materials and vernacular style. While the main structural walls were made of local stone, and referenced the fieldstone walls of the surrounding rural countryside, the secondary walls overlooking the inner courtyard were ceiling-to-floor glass in steel frames. In Noyes's words, the house is "a fortress on one side and all glass on the other."

Noyes was among the first to incorporate glass walls in a house (as opposed to large picture windows), and to so completely blend interior and exterior living spaces. Yet each space had a clearly defined purpose: one side of the structure had the bedrooms and bathrooms, the other the main living space. The inner courtyard was sparsely planted with one flowering tree shading a sculpture, while the house was sited within the existing landscape, the vertical lines of the surrounding trees counterpointing the lean and low horizontal of the house. (To reach the bathrooms from the main living area one had to cross the open courtyard—a quick dash in winter—but that, too, served to blur the boundaries.)

The house could hardly have been more simple: Noyes himself referred to it as "a very hard-boiled piece of architecture." It was also the first of what he called his "wall houses," inspired by medieval hillside villages in Italy, France, and Greece, where narrow streets are tightly bordered by the façades of houses that are cantilevered at the back over hillside slopes. In designing houses using this model (including a ski house in Vermont that he built for his family), Noyes tied the structure ever more tightly to its landscape, and, in a nod to the early forms of modernism, also adopted Frank Lloyd Wright's "desert concrete" to build the stone walls, because, as he noted, suitable stone was often difficult to find, and stonemasons were expensive.

On the East Coast, the evolution of a house fully integrated with the landscape can be traced in the architectural enclave at New Canaan, Connecticut. Eliot Noyes, an industrial designer, famously known for his design work for IBM and Mobil Oil, designed this house for his family. Fortress-like from one aspect, see-through from another, the glass and stone elevations enclose an inner courtyard, but seamlessly incorporate the structure into the woodland.

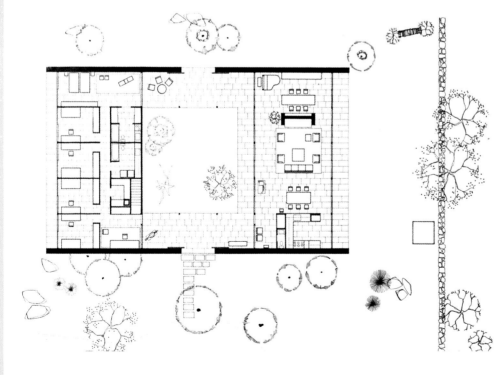

Canadian landscape architect, Christopher Tunnard, came to prominence in America in the 1940s. But between the wars, Tunnard had been in England and actively involved in helping to define the role of landscape architects in the context of modernism. He was particularly engaged with a Belgian landscape architect, Jean Canneel-Claes, in formulating a professional organization to address the need for landscape practitioners to define themselves as separate from nurserymen, surveyors, horticulturists and allied trades, but most especially as a being a profession separate from, but partner to, architects. When Le Corbusier pronounced that the "outside is always an inside" the landscape profession's territory was co-opted, and landscape architects feared being deprived of not only their identity but their *raison d'etre*. Architects formed an exclusive club and in some instances—among the French architects— prevented landscapers from using the hallowed "A" word in their professional title. It would seem that it was all in a name, and the appellation was quickly losing its meaning.

The identity crisis, however, did nothing to stop the general feeling that a new way had to be found to shape the rebuilding of a landscape devastated by the First World War.

A modern way to garden

Every country in northern Europe had been impacted by the Great War, and nationalism was perceived by many to be the root cause. In Belgium, Canneel was among the first in his profession to promote the need for a new "modern" approach to gardens, private and public, and to redefine the language of landscape, just as architecture was finding a new direction with the emergence of Bauhaus and the International Style. In time, and allied with Tunnard and other landscapers, the idea evolved that there should be no national boundaries in landscape design: no "English" landscape parks, no "French" parterres and so forth. Nor should there be any identifiable stylistic, historic patterns to design; medieval knot gardens, gothic grottoes. The modern way was to allow functionality to prevail, and from that form would follow; there being few differences among cultures of the experience a garden was expected to deliver. Function was fairly universal—recreation, relaxation and rejuvenation. But form allowed for some degree of interpretation, and in the case of the garden, where regional variations of climate and habitat were systemic, the beauty of nature as represented by plants and their various forms was accepted.

The first conference, convened in Brussels in 1934, was hosted by the *Association Belge des Architectes de Jardins* (Belgian Association of Garden Architects). Members attending included Pietro Porcinai from Italy, Ulla Bodorff from Sweden, and Achille Duchêne of France. This was followed in 1937 by a meeting in Paris of the first International Congress of Garden Architects. In 1938, the *Association Internationale des Architectes Jardinistes Modernistes* (International Association of Modernist Garden Architects) was established. In the last two Tunnard played an important role as the quasi-official

LANDSCAPE AND PLANTSMANSHIP IN ENGLAND AND EUROPE

Plantsmanship was never off the agenda in European landscape design. In Britain, especially, and at gardens like Buscot Old Parsonage in Oxfordshire, *opposite*, designed by Brenda Colvin (see also page 53), the blending of the natural with the designed introduced the postwar modernist garden ideal.

commentator; his remarks at the conclusion of the international conference were broad in their summing up, advising professionals to "reject old ways," and to become more relevant to modern life by "the use of logic and sanity and a poetic interpretation for the needs of society." Tunnard was known for his articles on the practicalities of popular gardening, but after this his writings targeted professionals and, in 1938, were compiled into a book, titled *Gardens in the Modern Landscape.* He wrote, in the chapter titled, "Toward a New Technique," that "The fact that garden making is in part a science does not free it from the duty of performing an aesthetic function; it can no more be turned over to the horticulturist than architecture to the engineer." And, "The modern house requires modern surrounding, and in most respects the garden of today does not fulfill this need."

In 1938, the International Congress of Garden Architects was held in Berlin, against a tense political backdrop. The old guard traditionalists and progressive modernists joined a conference that was in large part a stage for German nationalist propaganda. It is interesting to note that the German contingent presented their ideal for road-building—a winding road that followed the existing contours of the landscape—as preferable to the straight, or Latin, road, the sort built by the Romans. They regarded this as an artificial conceit because straight lines are never found in nature. One has to wonder if the Germans were aware that they were basing their approach to autobahn planning on the principles of an Englishman who had been inspired by French painters: "Nature abhors a straight line," is the *mot* expressed by William Kent, an early eighteenth-century English landscape designer, who, inspired by the work of French artists Claude Lorrain and Nicolas Poussin, shaped the great landscape park at Stowe, England, complete with meandering paths through sculpted "natural" landscapes decorated with structures modeled on the monuments of classical architecture.

At the 1938 conference, Jens Jensen numbered among the presenters as well as the Swedish landscape architect, Sven Hermelin. Hermelin, like Jensen, abandoned the rigid structure of the formal plan and instead turned his attention to nature and the native landscape to inspire his work. In 1934, he came to the conclusion that the strength of Swedish gardens was that they faced outwards. He wrote, "...so much more is offered by our countryside that the task of the landscape architect becomes a matter of *carefully integrating the building with the existing site conditions and arranging the transitional zone between the two* [author's italics]."

Where many European cultures viewed the wild as a threatening place to be tamed or dominated, for Swedes, the natural landscape was a health-giving, inviting and friendly environment in which they could be entirely at home. For them, the outside had long been the inside, to paraphrase Le Corbusier. And Hermelin, early on in his career, evolved his consultancy practice from directing historic garden restorations to championing the "wild" as an hospitable space in which to live and garden. Like Jensen, he was attuned to the subtleties of nature's language; one of his favorite criticisms was,

"THE TASK OF THE LANDSCAPE ARCHITECT BECOMES A MATTER OF CAREFULLY INTEGRATING THE BUILDING WITH THE EXISTING SITE CONDITIONS AND ARRANGING THE TRANSITIONAL ZONE BETWEEN THE TWO"

Opposite, St. Ann's Court in Chertsey, England is a modernist house designed in 1936 by Raymond McGrath. The landscape was designed by Christopher Tunnard, whose home it was. Tunnard reworked the late eighteenth-century park to include more functional modern features, like a swimming pool, and sweeping terraces for entertaining.

MODERN INFLUENCES FROM SCANDINAVIA

In his presentation, Tunnard quotes three lengthy paragraphs from a paper delivered by the President of the Swedish Garden Architects Association at the 1937 conference mentioned earlier. Before embarking Tunnard notes admiringly that the paper is a group effort and not one person's manifesto, which, of course, his own book published the following year was.

"Ordinarily," he quotes the Swedish paper, "the garden is planned in such a way as to form a direct relationship with the house, access from one to the other being everywhere facilitated. The garden thus becomes part of the dwelling. Its arrangement is decided more for the activities of people— especially children—than for flowers." Paths are reduced to stepping stones set in creeping groundcover plants so that they blend easily with paved areas for seating that here and there punctuate sweeping (often unmown) lawns. Flowering shrubs are preferred over trees; perennials have dedicated areas for their cultivation (the plants chosen as being suited to site).

The building's utilitarian style is better complemented by an asymmetrically planned garden, so formality in design is a thing of the past, and contrast between the rigid forms of walls and hardscaping and the "free and luxuriant vegetation designed to produce a happy decorative effect and to give the impression that is a work of nature or of chance." The effect of an existing gnarled pine or a group of trees should be used to counterpoint the "smooth walls of the house," in courtyards, individual plants should be encouraged to grow between pavers "to give the impression that they have grown there spontaneously." Yet this last paragraph pains Tunnard; despite the fact that the Swedes, as he perceives it, are capable of evolving a simple language for their garden architecture, one that is almost devoid of stylistic rhetoric, they have been unable to leave behind their "romantic conception of Nature." But he admits at the end that most of us can't take too much of nature unadorned, and need to have a garden around the house, "planned in accordance with human needs."

Functionalism was and remains a key factor in the success of Scandinavian design and lifestyle. Their practical approach to creating simple, rational products is a response, perhaps, to their environment and their geographical separation from the mainstream in European design and manufacture. Winters are long and dour, summer is brief and exquisite, and demands respect and celebration. Meadow gardens planted with only the lightest human touch complement interiors that are warm and bright, made comfortable by furnishings that are simple, elegant and often hand-crafted. Even in the early 20th-century building codes, there was a regard for nature: for many years buildings could not be constructed taller than the treetops.

Scandinavian design speaks eloquently to human needs, and its appeal has translated through the decades, from the early through the mid 20th-century, through the popular Conran/Habitat of 1970s Britain to the 21st-century global appeal of Ikea: functional, simple, fun, and carrying a timelessness that appeals to moderns, young and old.

Below left, a C. Th. Sørensen-designed garden in Denmark shows his more structured approach to landscaping. *Below right*, Swedish architect Per Friberg's home in Ljunghusen. *Opposite*, Noormarkku, designed by Finnish architect Alva Aalto in the late 1930s.

"that looks as if it were planted, it is supposed to look like it grows." And, like Jensen, he was consciously striving to bring the healing strength of nature into his landscape plans, and in this respect was a staunch advocate for the creation of public parks and open space as a social benefit. Where, in the early 1900s, Jensen was creating public parks to benefit Chicago's urban working class, in 1937, Hermelin undertook one of his most significant projects, creating a park at the Marabou chocolate factory as recreational space to benefit factory workers. And by the midcentury one of his residential projects set the course for Scandinavian garden design: his 1945 forest-edge landscape for the Markelius house was innovative in the way it took prominence over the house. But note the utilitarian kitchen garden laid out in traditional formal plan, the one area in which human intervention is seemingly most concentrated.

The International Congress of Landscape Architects convened what would be its final meeting in Zurich on the eve of the Second World War. Notable absentees were Jean Canneel and Christopher Tunnard, who left England on the day Germany invaded Poland, 1 September 1939. He made his way to the United States and an academic career at Harvard Graduate School of Design, on the urging of landscape architect Dan Kiley and modernist architect Philip Johnson, among others. Tunnard's advocacy for landscape architecture never ceased, and he continued through his writing and teaching to emphasize the relevance of the practice in the public realm and to promote it as an equal collaborator with architecture.

Swedish landscape architect Sven Hermelin's highly livable landscapes, such as the one he designed for the Markelius family home shown here, celebrated the garden and living with nature—something he saw as key to leading a healthy life. The plan *below* shows produce gardens, terraces and recreation spaces integrated with the natural landscape as well as the house and outbuildings.

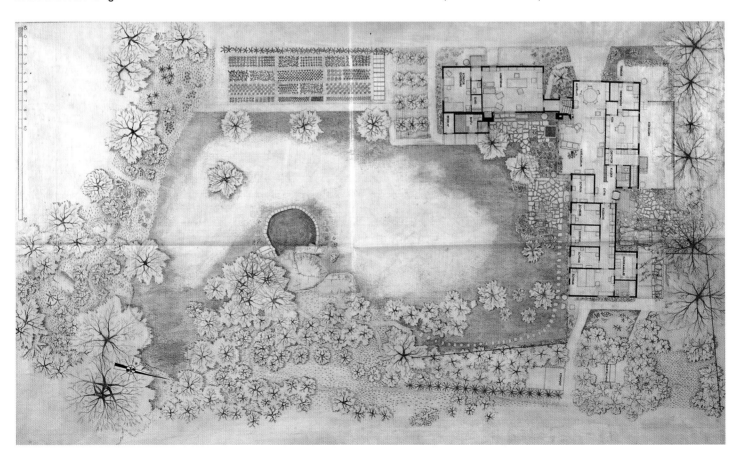

The trial gardens at Weihenstephan, Germany, *below* and *opposite,* were developed in the interwar period by Richard Hansen. He wrote, "The success of a perennial planting invariably depends on a proper appreciation of the given ecological conditions and the chosen plants' ecological requirements." Hansen went on to say that ultimately, even though an architect may have designed the garden, the perennial plantings are best left to a gardener.

But what of the plantsmen who had been active supporters of the natural or wild garden? The war in Europe ended in 1945, with Karl Foerster cut off from the mainstream, in East Germany. However, a number of devoted followers were committed to carrying on his plant selection programs and to developing his ideas of harmonizing art and nature in the garden. Chief among them was Richard Hansen, whose pre-war studies included time spent cataloguing and indexing native plants, and as a result had a sound grasp of how plant communities evolved and coexisted to their mutual benefit. This was the foundation for the development, in 1947, of his trial gardens at the University of Weihenstephan in Bavaria. Believing that plant types, existing in "manmade plant communities" (i.e., trees, shrubs, perennials, bulbs) could not be considered in isolation, but should be treated as an integrated system, he planted trial borders and beds accordingly. He explained, "A trial means selecting the best cultivars and species [... as well as] the correct site or habitat for a plant and, in ecological terms, suitable companion plants [...] Harmony and beauty need space and our environment should be infiltrated with life. The diversity of nature should be recognizable in each green space or border." The Weihenstephan gardens and Hansen's book, *Perennial Plants and Their Garden Habitats* (1981), which codifies plant communities for nearly every imaginable situation—from deep, damp shade to exposed, dry sun—continue as valuable resources for designers

gardeners around the world, and have had an enormous impact on current trends in landscape and garden design.

Between the years 1933 and 1951, from an office in Hillier House, Guildford, Surrey, Theo A. Stephens the publisher and editor of a small format gardening magazine, *My Garden,* collaborated with some of England's most respected horticulturists, plant collectors and gardening authors to produce his gently lyrical and clearly upmarket journal aimed at the remnants of the upper class and landed gentry. Subtitled *An Intimate Magazine for Garden Lovers* his target audience tended their "grounds" themselves now that gardeners and household retainers were a thing of the past thanks to the ravages of the First World War. Nevertheless, these privileged few were more interested in increasing their rockery plants collections than producing carrots and cabbages.

In the October 1936 issue, Stephens wrote, "Politically and economically speaking the world, and Europe in particular, is in a ghastly mess." Citing the Spanish Civil War, Stephens, in a note of guarded optimism, offered his opinion that a similar situation would be unlikely to happen in Britain, where more people [referring to the expanding suburban middle class] owned houses, and many had a garden, which in fact made them even less likely to "join the ranks of the malcontents." Fifteen years later, as he prepared to print his last issue of *My Garden,* Stephens sounded ready to join the ranks himself, lamenting that he could not get decent coal for his fire, paper for his magazine was in short supply and, worse, the

magazine, for the first time since its inception, had not sold out its issue. "Looking at things from my own personal standpoint," he wrote, "I and those of my particular class, have had our day and we shall never get back to the *status quo ante bellum*—the first or the second."

The English garden declines

Life in England was on the ropes, no doubt: the sun had set on the luxurious homes and gardens of the Edwardian Golden Afternoon, and rose again only to shine upon economic downturn, political unrest and sabre-rattling across the channel. It shone ever so briefly on a country trying to hold onto its architectural and landscape heritage: post First World War, even the Edwin Lutyens manor houses set in expansive and expensive Gertrude Jekyll gardens, that had been built for *nouveau riche* industrialists and minor nobility, were slowly sinking into decay.

Up to that point, there really had not been any garden style that could be identified as purely English since the great landscaped parks of the eighteenth century, when William Kent and Capability Brown and others recognized the potential (or "capabilities") of the English landscape and set out to "improve" it. As noted earlier, the pendulum of style swung back and forth between creating garden pictures of formal historicism and gardens where nature was revered and wildness prevailed, albeit with a fair bit of help from the improving hand of the gardener.

All that changed with the influx of new plant material from the far reaches of the British Empire and North America. Plantsmanship and gardens created for colorful displays of choice perennials, bulbs, shrubs and trees became the ideal garden for English gardeners from all walks of life. Gardeners became plant collectors, and the garden was no longer a work of art but a horticultural trial ground. Between the wars, generally speaking, the gardener's considerations of design and plan were subjugated to the cultural needs of the plants being grown.

For at least ten years post-Second World War, there were greater considerations than the finer points of gardening and landscape design. The bombed out populations of major urban centers like London, Birmingham and Coventry demanded housing and employment. Fast and efficient construction was required to house as many people as possible as quickly as possible, while industry had urgently to re-tool for peacetime production. Some economists determine that Britain did not make the best of the Marshall Plan; rationing continued until well into the 1950s, so food production remained a prime concern. Vegetable gardens took precedence over herbaceous borders.

Tower blocks and concrete were the quick fix for housing a displaced population, and food production did indeed take precedence over fine gardening. But that doesn't mean that landscape architects faded into the shrubbery. Far from it: just as European designers had been organizing during the 1920s,

so British designers had been organizing to define a national style. In landscape design it led to the formation of the Institute of Landscape Architects in 1929. Chief among its early members were Russell Page, Geoffrey Jellicoe, Brenda Colvin and later, Sylvia Crowe. Post-war, they were instrumental in moving the business of landscape architecture out of the private realm of pleasure gardens into a collaborative role with new town planners and architects to create meaningful spaces for public amenity.

Birth of the Modern

In her important 1958 book, *Garden Design*, Sylvia Crowe explained that the emerging style of American contemporary domestic gardens ultimately had its roots in the English landscaped parks of the 1700s, filtered through a layer of styles including the naturalistic "wild" gardens of the early 1900s and the cottagesque gardens of Jekyll and Robinson. From this arose a "recognizable type of garden, associated particularly with Scandinavia, remarkable for its domestic quality and its deceptive air of casualness." She praises these prototypes for their comfort, simplicity and "sensitivity to organic growth" and qualifies them as important because "they set a standard of attainable excellence for the small and modest garden."

Between the wars, Geoffrey Jellicoe rose rapidly in stature as a forward-thinking landscape architect and town planner, garden designer, lecturer and author. There is not space here to recount his many achievements, but suffice to say that Jellicoe's philosophy, grounded in a profound understanding of the importance of landscape history and informed by Jungian analysis, was disseminated through major international projects and his many books. *The Landscape of Man: Shaping the Environment from Prehistory to the Present Day*, published in 1975, served as a visual guide to what was appropriate in a garden. It had been preceded in 1968 by Jellicoe's *Modern Private Gardens,* a book that featured the work of some forty gardens throughout the United States and Europe, created by contemporary designers at the top of their field such as Lanning Roper, Pietro Porcinai, Walter Bauer, Garrett Eckbo, Thomas Church, John Brookes, Sylvia Crowe and Brenda Colvin.

In his introduction to this collection of small gardens, curated by him to be visually different and to lead from enclosed intimate gardens to wide open landscapes, Jellicoe observed that gardens were geographically separated into those of the eastern or the western hemispheres: gardens in the west "arose through fear of the environment," while those in the east came about for reasons that were "precisely the opposite." And an appreciation of this was key to the success of modern gardens as the two cultural traditions were amalgamating. Historically, in the west, the land was there to be tamed by the will of mankind; in the east landscape was revered.

The pool garden at Cottesbrooke Manor, Northamptonshire, England, *opposite*, was a garden addition designed in the mid-1950s by Sylvia Crowe. Its air of unforced simplicity replaced a fussy rose garden from an earlier era.

The stark concrete stacks of the University of East Anglia, designed by Denys Lasdun in the 1960s were softened by Brenda Colvin's sensitive landscaping around the Broad, a natural water feature common in Norfolk. Colvin improved the wetland habitat around the Broad, making it a serviceable area for students' recreation.

FROM THIS AROSE A "RECOGNIZABLE TYPE OF GARDEN, ASSOCIATED PARTICULARLY WITH SCANDINAVIA, REMARKABLE FOR ITS DOMESTIC QUALITY AND ITS DECEPTIVE AIR OF CASUALNESS"

The modern garden, Jellicoe wrote, was now a small and physically confined space, where "...man is now absorbed in creating whole worlds in which the imagination can adventure. Perhaps above all he is seeking to escape from the world of bricks and mortar into a primitive disordered world of his own." And to enable this escape, *content* and *form* offer the key.

Within a garden, the *content* (the plants, ornaments and furnishings), being more obvious, should have some over-arching theme to ensure that they cohere to each other and the form of the garden. The content should express the owner's preferences, but also those of the plants, the choice of which should respond to the site.

In Jellicoe's language, *form* was the modeling of the space in which the *content* was deployed. How these two elements were manipulated resulted in a uniquely personal expression. In his practice, small gardens in particular were inward-looking spaces, their form best shaped by the owner's personal preferences rather by than by a slavish adherence to outmoded historical rules. Interestingly, Jellicoe believed that abstract art (Paul Klee was one with whom he particularly identified) and garden design had much in common because both offered the subconscious mind freedom to express itself through the shapes and compositions that "it craves," and ultimately find satisfaction.

In his understanding of the small modern garden, Jellicoe folds a heady blend of natural science, art history and philosophy, and psychology. Our response to landscape, he once remarked to me, is buried in our archetypal understanding of nature as a living force. The closing quote to his introduction is an eloquent expression of change as it manifested in the mid-twentieth century:

"And this our life, exempt from public haunt,
Finds tongues in trees, books in the running brooks,
Sermons in stones, and good in everything."

William Shakespeare, *As You Like It* (II, i)

Left, Sir Geoffrey Jellicoe at his drawing desk in 1990. Describing his process to me, he commented that he knew "nothing about plants," which was his wife Susan's "department."

Below, *The Bird Garden* (1910)—one of a series of garden paintings by Paul Klee. A Bauhaus teacher, he believed that art knew no boundaries; that multiple realities existed within the human psyche and were expressed by the arts.

At Shute House in Dorset, England, Jellicoe developed what he called the "waterscape," drawing inspiration from 2,000 years of garden history and the notable presence of water. Harnessing an abundance of water from the surrounding springs, The Rill, *opposite*, directs it over a series of cascades, intended to mimic the musical range (alto, treble, tenor and bass) of the male voice. These sorts of *giochi d'acqua* (water jokes) were very popular in Italian gardens during the eighteenth century.

At the end of the Second World War there was expectation in some quarters that the United States would descend into recession as it had after the First World War. Government expenditure at the end of the Second World War dropped 80 per cent, from a 1944 high of $135 billion to $25 billion (in 1951 prices), and demobilization happened quickly, yet there was no recession—this time the government was prepared. Not only was there a speedy repurposing of industry and manufacturing, from creating weapons of war to arming the public with a vast new array of consumer goods, but veterans could draw unemployment compensation while they job-hunted, or receive grants to complete their education. Government-guaranteed, low-interest bank loans available through the G.I. Bill were available to veterans so that they could set up businesses or buy houses. Individuals' savings were high while their private debt was low, and this, combined with a desire to spend on now readily available and affordable products (chiefly automobiles), soon put manufacturing on a road to peacetime prosperity, creating jobs which in turn encouraged an increase in consumer spending.

Austerity was a thing of the past and growth was the goal, although economic forecasters urged caution, worried that employment would not keep up and spending would suffer. They were quickly proved wrong. Once the wheels of the peacetime bus started turning, consumers piled on board, as one economist observed, "buying whatever they could lay their hands on." With little to spend their money on during the war years, people's savings grew.

Economists predicted that people would resume saving at pre-war levels. They were wrong. But post-war debt, chiefly in the form of mortgages and car loans, grew sharply. Recovering from World War Two, people were filled with optimism and a determination to make up for lost time, and to spend, spend, spend.

The good life

The post-war growth expressed itself in a drive to reach out toward new frontiers, particularly in the way life was lived. The idea of the good life held the greatest allure, and for many that equated broadly with the west, specifically with Southern California. In 1887, Santa Fe railways completed the final link in their transcontinental connection to Los Angeles, eventually making it a destination for tourists, many of whom—particularly those from the Midwest—were determined to make it their new home. One railway official predicted the area would soon become "one of the most densely populated sections of the United States." The developers were not far behind them: within two years some 80,000 acres around Los Angeles had been turned into sixty new towns. And despite the property bubble bursting, the migration westward continued.

And why wouldn't these optimistic, hard-working Midwesterners forsake the climate extremes of the prairies? The weather in Southern California was even and mild, and the air was clean and sweet with the perfume of citrus orchards. Most alluringly for people seeking to escape the cheek-by-jowl density of the east,

WEST COAST MODERNISM AND OUTDOOR LIVING

Opposite, a low-slung ranch house makes the most of the West Coast's balmy climate for outdoor living. Located in West Los Angeles and designed and built in 1956 by Cliff May for his family, it blended the best attributes of old Spanish colonial ranch houses with new concepts in easy living. The surrounding gardens were designed by Thomas Church to specific purposes, including a dining terrace, a social terrace and children's play area, all of which related to the layout of the rooms of the house. It has been the prototype for houses like it built all over the world.

there was plenty of space to spread out. Single-family homes were the norm for those of even the most modest means. Between the wars, Los Angeles was a boomtown that attracted an influx of working class families to serve industry, as well as Dust Bowl refugees who brought their farming skills to Southern California's expanding agriculture. The result was a property shortage that by the mid-1930s had become acute. To meet it, builders adapted their craftsman-built approach to that of the production line: Taylorism entered the construction business, and simple, quick-to-construct boxes became the norm. Dropped onto mown grass lawns and anchored by foundation plantings of mixed evergreen shrubs, they were differentiated one from the other by applied ornament in a variety of styles   from Renaissance Italian, to half-timbered Olde England.

Up to that point, the Arts and Crafts bungalow had been the preferred style for homebuilders and buyers. Staged against a formal setting of lawns, neatly clipped shrubs and tidy flower beds, broad porches beneath deep overhangs approached flights of steps. These led to large hallways and a series of well-ventilated, clearly purposed rooms—living room, dining room, bedrooms, etc. Often the property was spacious enough to harbor a few orange trees and other ornamentals.

Houses for ordinary people

East Coast and mittel-European modernism was also staking out ground in California: Austrian-American architects Rudolph Schindler and Richard Neutra were, by the mid-1920s, advancing the use of plate glass and steel frame construction to help average, middle-income homeowners make the most of the Californian climate. Frank Lloyd Wright was present, too. However, the new wave modernists' avant-garde ideas of social welfare expressed through architecture did not generate popular appeal. Their designs became the preserve of more well-to-do private clients who bought into the modernist intellectual principles and notions of form and function. This may be dismissing their work in too offhand a manner, but their ideals of creating efficient and inspiring housing for the greater good, and for the toiling masses, was more effectively realized later on. The years after the Second World War saw the evolution of the ranch house style, as promoted most noticeably by the work of builder and developer Cliff May, who began his career as an architectural designer. From 1932, when he built his first ranch house, until his death in 1989, May built affordable, livable houses that ordinary people could imagine living in. These were homes, not concepts. His inspiration came from the traditional Spanish-influenced haciendas of old California. Born and raised in San Diego, May had firsthand knowledge of the vernacular. With their rooms arranged around a central courtyard, and open planning advantageous to cross-ventilation, May believed that "the basic old California plan, seemed to be a much better way to build and live." All the fresh-to-the-scene architects, May opined, who were espousing the importance of functional architecture expressed in native building materials, were

"THE BASIC OLD CALIFORNIA PLAN, SEEMED TO BE A MUCH BETTER WAY TO BUILD AND LIVE"

The entranceway to a Beverly Hills house designed by A. Quincy Jones for the Hollywood actor, Gary Cooper. Jones, who also worked with the developer Joseph Eichler building his iconic tract homes in Southern California, designed this house specifically to fit his client's needs for a house that was thoroughly modern, but which in its materials reflected Cooper's traditional values and love of the West. The original landscape was designed by Garrett Eckbo and included a vegetable garden and an indoor/outdoor water feature. When the house was completed in the mid-1950s, Cooper commented that it was so advanced in design that he wondered if they were living in the year 2000.

not onto something new: "all of the old California architecture was built that way—functional. The only building material they had was what they dug out of the ground."

In these ranch houses, the scale of the building was determined by the length of the wood they cut; the door opened directly onto the patio, there were no steps to interrupt the flow, and windows were positioned to maximize ventilation. This became May's criteria as he developed the California ranch style, from the G.I. Ranch House in the 1930s to the Robert Mondavi Winery and its accompanying home in the 1980s. Looking back over his long career, May commented to the interviewer of an oral history, "I only built one kind of house." But that covered more than 1,000 homes and commercial structures, and included the use of his house plans, which he licensed to other builders, for the construction of more than 18,000 ranch-style houses in tract development from California to Connecticut, Ireland to Australia. He built economical, efficient family homes for the working man as well as vast spreads for captains of industry, but the principles, cited above, remained the same. He did not build boxes, and disdained the Irving Gill style of squares within squares. His homes rambled around a central courtyard, or in smaller homes "We had garages out front. We had a lot of inducements [for the small homebuyer] like covered pergolas, or *ramadas* [...] and floor-to-ceiling window entrances screened by carports, and trellis arbors shading patios and walkways [...] Patios, courtyards and trees." And all at the right price for the time, post-Second World War. Cliff May's

In California, the easy-going lifestyle made possible by the climate ensured that no home could be considered modern without an atrium, which could often be one of the main rooms. Cliff May was well known for his open ridge beam design and the interior of his experimental Skylight House, *opposite* and *above*, could be shaded by a sail-type awning pulled across the opening.

RESISTANCE TO MODERNISM

Most homebuyers resisted the idea of modernist houses built in the "Miesian" style, or that of the venerated Corbu, try as some architectural critics might to promote them as a popular choice. The Case Study houses, commissioned by John Entenza, the publisher of an upscale design magazine *Arts and Architecture,* led to the construction, between 1945 and 1966, of a number of houses by important modernist architects including Charles and Ray Eames, Richard Neutra, Eero Saarinen, William Wurster and others. The most widely recognized is the Stahl House, CSH #22, built in 1960 and designed by Pierre Koenig. Perched on an overlook above Los Angeles, it is as iconic a piece of architecture as Frank Lloyd Wright's famous Fallingwater.

During the time that these exhilarating exercises in modernism were being promoted, Cliff May (not invited to contribute to the program) was enjoying his own promotion through the pages of *House Beautiful*, a distinctly down-to-earth shelter magazine that commissioned a series of ranch houses from May, hailing them as the new architecture for the new way of living. May recalled his special relationship with the *House Beautiful* editor Elizabeth Gordon and her husband, both of whom he knew to be well educated, well traveled and with tastes that, while sophisticated, were grounded in reality. When, at one point, May tried to get one of his designs for a large ranch house published (his own home, Mandalay, actually), Gordon refused. "Frankly," she said, "it's just too big. You can't have a living room fifty-five feet long and furnish it [...] How would you furnish Grand Central Station? [...] It's just out of the reach and comprehension of our readership."

And therein lay the key to May's popular success—he could go big when commissioned to do so, but the bulk of his output was within reach of a wide audience, while the Miesian modernist's homes appealed to a more rarefied market.

Architect Pierre Koenig realizes the vision of his client Buck Stahl for a hillside site overlooking Los Angeles. Built in 1960 as a Case Study House, the benign parking forecourt, *opposite above*, belies the electrifying architectural drama beyond. In response to the spectacular site, there is no garden space to speak of other than a pool terrace, but the urban landscape of Los Angeles perhaps makes one unnecessary, *opposite below*. An earlier Koenig house built in 1955, *below,* was by contrast a secluded but open-sided cabin in the woods, surrounded on all sides by flowering shrubs and sheltering trees; absorbed by and at one with nature.

plans were based on the idea of enclosed space. "The whole California way of living," he said, "is for protection and for trapping the sun and for having privacy." And who doesn't want that?

Cliff May was not alone as a designer of tract-built housing; there were many—too many to name here. But among the most prominent were William Krisel, whose first tract of butterfly-roofed houses with patio-edged pools and sweeps of plate glass set the style for desert homes from Palm Springs to Las Vegas, and A. Quincy Jones and Joseph Stein (architect of Ladera, an experimental cooperative housing development near Palo Alto); both worked for Joseph Eichler, a developer whose homes are much sought after today. But where May's houses were cast in the easy-going long and low style of old California, Eichler homes spoke to an optimistic vision of the future. Their rooflines soar up and out like jet wings, and have deep overhangs to shade glass walls, which combined with plant-filled atriums, blend and blur notions of what interior and exterior space can be.

In Europe, landscape modernists may have been frustrated in their attempts to gain professional recognition, and to be seen as on a par with architects working in mutually agreeable design partnerships, (to the extent that Henri Pasquier remarked to his landscape colleagues, "Let's design green spaces while no one is looking,") but the opposite was true in the United States, and especially so in California. As individual homes and tract-built developments went up, the architects and developers worked with an array of stellar landscape and garden designers to ensure that the houses were set in complementary gardens; that they made the best use of site and existing plants; and that, for the higher-end dwellings, the landscape was the perfect setting for their architectural jewel, and vice versa.

In common with their architect partners, there were landscape architects and designers who reached for revolutionary solutions to domestic landscape. But while these homes and gardens may have matured into landmarks of design, off the drawing board they were beyond the comprehension of the average prospective homebuyer at that time. This buyer was looking for stability, tranquility and easy care to match their new low-key, sunny California lifestyle. Returning to Cliff May, his G.I. Ranch House served as a prototype. Built in 1945, it was 1,000 square feet, had a carport attached to the front (to show off the new family car), an open plan living area with skylights, and sliding glass doors onto a patio. The building materials were nothing fancy, just board and batten, and it was erected on a concrete slab. As May explained, he wanted people to be able to access the ground without a change in levels, "if you have to go down steps, you're not living like a real Californian lives from the house to the patio. You can't get a tie or continuity or a relation to the garden if you are looking down steps at it. I call it, 'ground contact.'" This intimate association between the interior and exterior remained when May's practice became more centered on bespoke construction of large homes. In either case, a May-built ranch house

EICHLER HOMES SPOKE TO AN OPTIMISTIC VISION OF THE FUTURE. THEIR ROOFLINES SOAR UP AND OUT LIKE JET WINGS, AND HAVE DEEP OVERHANGS TO SHADE GLASS WALLS, WHICH COMBINED WITH PLANT-FILLED ATRIUMS, BLEND AND BLUR NOTIONS OF WHAT INTERIOR AND EXTERIOR SPACE CAN BE

An experimental house designed by the Italian-born architect Pietro Belluschi was just one of many programmatic houses constructed in the early postwar era to generate mass-market appeal for new concepts in design. Designed to cost less than $25,000, it featured a cantilevered deck to enhance the outdoor experience in response to a modest homeowner's desire for a taste of avant-garde landscape theater.

Cliff May's 1945 design for the prototype "G.I. Ranch House," *above,* brought together all the elements for comfortable modern living—indoors and out—at a bargain price. It became the popular housing format nationwide.

With his book, *Gardens are For People,* California landscape designer Thomas Church laid the ground rules for the American ideal of outdoor living: respect for the site, the need for simplicity, and whenever possible, the inclusion of a swimming pool, as in his design for the Donnelly house garden, *right.*

offered many of the same features, or "inducements" as he called them: "pergolas, or *ramadas* we called them in Spanish, walls and baffles and floor-to-ceiling windows."

Comfortable outdoor lifestyle

While ranch houses epitomized the easy-going elegance of midcentury modern living, the gardens of Thomas Dolliver Church, also known as Tommy Church, were what everybody wanted to ensure their outdoor lifestyle was as comfortable as their indoor one. With his 1955 book, *Gardens are for People,* Church provided middle-class suburban homeowners with a guide to creating simple gardens that were low on maintenance but high on style, even given their limited space. This was often less than a quarter of an acre, divided into a formal front yard (the public face of a private home), narrow side yard—often not more than a shadowed narrow passage between houses—and a back yard accessed through the utility rooms, which often dictated the use of the limited outdoor space: an area for laundry lines, a straight pathway to the alley access for trash removal. Church understood his audience and was able to create another vision of what might be. "You cannot," he wrote in the chapter "Design Principles," "have all the gardens you have clipped from the pages of *House Beautiful* and *Arts and Architecture.*" He had precise recommendations: if the house has a step or steps down into the garden, see if a window from one of the main rooms can

Visiting Europe in 1937, Church met Alvar Aalto and the experience altered his approach to design, which became more focused on the use of site and line than on plants. The sculpture in the Donnelly pool, *left,* has a direct correlation to the contours of the landforms and the curvilinear pool itself.

In Church's design for a beachside residence in Aptos, California, *right,* a wooden gangway leading to the beach, banked by islands of greenery, sand and gravel, is turned to sculpture by a zigzag edging.

be converted to allow ground-level entry; next consider the functions of the garden space, and begin by establishing the "inevitable" utility areas, confining them to as small an area as possible placed "logically" near the service area of the house. "It is not wise to be overambitious in designing the garden. Too many things going on in a small area produces a restless quality." Marry the garden more closely to the house by using similar materials; consider a terrace as a transition between in and out of doors—and if space is extremely limited, "the whole area may be taken up with the garden terrace."

Church was not, however, in favor of doing without a lawn, regarding grass as an excellent groundcover and an island of visual calm against which the restrained planting he preferred was best displayed. Church urged the retention of old trees on a site to give a sense of age and permanence to a garden, and advised avoiding the sort of foundation planting that had been popular when houses had foundations, and which matured into evergreen shrouds overwhelming the architecture. In the modern era, when more and more houses were being built on slab foundations, it was best to move the plantings away from the house to take advantage of shadows and shade that would add texture and comfort to the landscape. Swimming pools were a forte, and his most famous house, the Donnelly, built for a wealthy private client, set the style for the curvilinear pool, seemingly sketched freehand, but in fact carefully composed

with a compass to ensure the curves corresponded to other site features. Attention to topography was critical, and where ground fell away or a tree made paved terracing impractical, he would specify a cantilevered wooden deck, positioning the planks around the tree trunks so they protruded like natural umbrellas to shade the decking.

Church's practice endured from the 1930s until 1977, when he retired. During those years he worked on projects great and small with some of the foremost landscape designers and architects in the US, including Lawrence Halprin, June Meehan and Roger Bayliss. His work was known internationally for its innovative embrace of modern style. Yet, as he explained in his introduction, "Landscaping is not a complex and difficult art to be practiced only by high priests [...] To weigh, advise, interpret, integrate, and come up with some answers beyond the ability and imagination of the layman is the role of the landscape architect."

Gardens that fit the landscape
Equally influential, but for different reasons, was the work of Garrett Eckbo, an ardent social activist and reformer, some eight years Church's junior, who approached landscape architecture as a means of social improvement. His book, *Landscape for Living,* published in 1950, set out his criteria for creating socially appropriate garden designs from the vantage point of their place within the greater landscape, rather than the needs of

Landscape architect Garrett Eckbo was a plantsman's landscape designer; for him there was no division between designing space and designing content. It was all one. In 1952 Eckbo designed the gardens of a new house built for the Nishi sisters, Kiyako and Miyako—nurserywomen who raised vegetable seedlings to sell to market growers. At the entrance, *above,* and in the garden behind the house, Eckbo married abstract shapes to exotic plant forms, creating a richly textured and exhilarating, complex garden. This and other gardens like it, *opposite,* were quite a contrast to the more restrained residential landscapes advocated by Tommy Church.

the individual homeowner. He presented solutions for "problems," writing that most planning discussions end with design and construction of the building, which is "only half the problem, and it must be tied in with the other half, the land-, site-, or garden-use problem, which completes the private home problem."

Eckbo talks about the modern house providing for the "mechanics of living" but lacking in provision for a complete environment. For this the modern house had to "extend into outdoor space" and be integrated with its environment. And yet the garden, which would provide this unity, had to be more and do more than simply provide a setting for outdoor living. "It must," he enthused, "like a bride, be perennially attractive, perennially gay, perennially delightful. Every visit to it must be an adventure and experience [...] Maximum delight, minimum maintenance; every detail right, every plant a specimen, every feature a thing of beauty and a joy forever."

Inspiring or daunting? Eckbo's advice reads at times like a manifesto for constructing landscapes for living, and couldn't be more different from Church's more avuncular suggestions for creating gardens for people. But this isn't so surprising. They were of different generations: though both were schooled at University of California, Berkeley, and did graduate degrees in landscape at Harvard. But Church retained in his work an element of the dignified formalism and aesthetic of the Beaux Arts school, while Eckbo, coming later to Harvard, when Beaux Arts was on the wane, found his place among the architects surrounding Walter Gropius, and

Eckbo's book, *Landscape for Living,* was his treatise on good design for home landscapes, directed at professionals. He wrote: "The free and creative organization of planes, masses, and structural patterns in space above the ground [and the] gamut of three-dimensional relations… is richer than any sterile axes, and 'informal' sprinkling or squiggling, that has been offered to date." And this principle he applied to spaces no matter how small, like the window well garden for the Johnson McFie house, *left,* or the Bolles residence, *below*.

Eckbo met the challenge of creating seemingly spacious gardens in small suburban lots by referencing the random organic shapes and rhythmic geometries of abstract impressionist painters, particularly Wassily Kandinsky and Paul Klee. In the confined space of the garden for the Koolish residence in Bel Air, *above* and *right,* Eckbo detracted attention from the boundary fence and encroaching rooflines of neighboring houses with a restless pattern of angles, circles and diagonals, making the space seem much larger than it

was, and infinitely more exciting than a traditional formal plan would have been. Yet it was formality that offered homeowners the relaxation they desired, and at the end of the day, it was Tommy Church's gardens—like his 1958 design for a pool terrace and garden at the Henderson house in Hillsborough, California, *overleaf*—that held the popular imagination.

so brought to his work the socialistic ideals expressed in the International Style. Where Church in his Harvard thesis looked at the adaptation of Mediterranean practice in garden design and horticulture to meet the needs of individual Californian gardens, Eckbo proposed in his, which he titled "Contempoville," a community in which residents had their own gardens, but shared in the use and upkeep of a community landscape. Indeed, following his graduation, Eckbo's first few projects, commissioned during the late 1930s by the Farm Security Administration, were to develop residential compounds for migrant agricultural workers. Later, in his work for private clients, Eckbo's modernism expressed itself in abstracted forms and modeling space, and in the use of avant-garde materials. For his own garden, Eckbo partnered with Alcoa to expand the boundaries of garden construction materials, while promoting a repurposing of a wartime material.

Just as ordinary people found the glass and steel boxes of the modernists less appealing than the ranch houses of Cliff May and other developers, so they found the quiet, simple gardens designed by Tommy Church easier to live with than they did Eckbo's bold experiments; today quite a few of Church's gardens still exist, while Eckbo's, with few exceptions, have all but disappeared. But just like popularity of the one-level, open plan ranch house has broad appeal, the American ideal of outdoor living has been grafted on to garden and landscape design all around the world.

MAKE IT MIDCENTURY

Midcentury modern style is about ease and comfort; furnishings are relaxed, *above*—a reflection of the "taking it easy" attitude that set the tone for the architectural and landscape style that emerged in the postwar years. Courtyard gardens, *opposite,* and poolside lounging areas, *right,* remain arenas for a personal expression of a new kind of living.

Previous page: An updated Eichler house sustains the midcentury ethos. The postwar years were optimistic and progressive: see-through living—the merging of exterior and interior spaces— expressed the promise of a bright future, and the time to enjoy life's simple pleasures.

INTRODUCTION

Deciding to embrace midcentury modern style is a bit like going on a diet. You know there are things you will have to give up, and others thing you will relish trying out. And there are all sorts of self-help books and magazines out there to advise you on how to go about it, how to succeed, and how to maintain the regime.

You can go the whole hog, and cleanse your surroundings of all items that are not pure and authentic, or decide that there is only so much you are willing to spend on acquiring period lawn chairs and opt for repro items that are within financial reach but still adhere to the midcentury modern aesthetic. Or, and I think this is the most interesting way to go, and the one most in keeping with the *thinking* of the period, you can look for contemporary,

well-designed items of modern craftsmanship. Don't forget, what is vintage midcentury modern now was new at the time. And stir in an artisan made tabletop or a few pieces of hand-woven or printed textiles. Looking closely at period photography, that was the blend. And what brought it to life was giving expression to the tastes of the homeowner.

The preceding can be applied as much to your outdoor space as to your indoor space. Because gardens of the time were really not *gardens* at all. They were frames for the houses, backdrops for living—created with a certain panache, of course. They were organized to be functional, unified spaces where the tool shed and the laundry line shared the stage with vivacious conversation

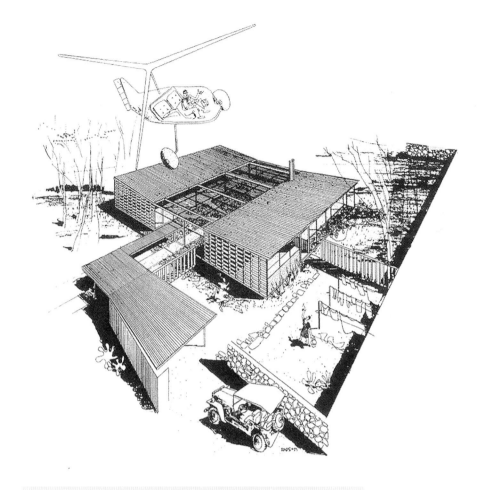

TO THE MANY, GARDENING WAS A CHORE, NOT AN ART. GARDENS WERE TO BE LIVED IN, NOT LOOKED AT

areas, serene lounging spots, cleverly shaped swimming pools and eating areas centered on the barbeque grill. All of these were necessary to the success of the midcentury modern garden (and more if space allowed: one has to put the croquet hoops somewhere!) Outdoor spaces would be woven together in free-flowing plans, and spot-lit by plant groupings or sculptural specimens that were attention getters, not collectors' pieces. Because, let it be understood right now, midcentury modern gardens are not about spending hours in the garden weeding the borders and dead-heading the perennials. A quick whizz around with the lawnmower, a clip over of the shrubs and the routine monitoring of the irrigation was generally all it took to keep the outdoor living space tidy. At least that is what became the prevalent model for North America—time not spent caring for the garden could be spent pursuing other interests. To the many, gardening was a chore, not an art. Gardens were to be lived in, not looked at.

Furthermore, in a culture that was and remains peripatetic—with families moving houses and states with every job move or upgrading homes with every life stage—it hardly seems worth planting a tree since one will have moved on before it gets its head up properly. This I know from personal experience, having moved three times in fifteen years since returning to the USA from England.

Futuristic design was encouraged by design competitions like the Case Study house series from the 1940s. Ralph Rapson's 1945 design for Case Study House #4, *opposite,* presented a glassed over atrium and a utility yard. The juxtaposition of the private helicopter and the Model T was a witty comment on the marriage of innovation and tradition. Although unbuilt, it was influential, and in California, the easy-going lifestyle made possible by the climate ensured that no home could be considered modern without an atrium.

Mobility was a byword for modern, and it was seen everywhere; from the automobile in every driveway, to the lightweight, easily portable furnishings such as the wire form garden furniture seen on this page. Preferred shapes hinted at the space age, as can be seen in bucket seats and satellite-shaped firepits.

The design tropes of midcentury style hold enormous appeal, even in climates that are cooler than those in California or the Mediterranean. The remodel of an Eichler-designed home, *above*, with its wall of glass, is a contemporary model for the blurring of interior and exterior space. The spaces are equal but separated by design: the Cubist-like geometry of the courtyard décor on this page distinguishes it from the softer, warmer mood of the interior.

Extending the roof to cover the patio, *opposite,* is another way to unite the living spaces; sections of the roof, both inside and out, are left open to flood the rooms with sunlight; the interior one is glazed, but the exterior is not. This was a favorite design feature in Cliff May houses.

In Britain, where the climate was less suited to outdoor living than it was in California, there was an ingrained disposition to gardening in all its forms. Midcentury modern landscaping was expressed in plants and how they were used to support the garden plan, rather than form it. Design became more relaxed and more attention was given to creating "wild" gardens, where plants were suited to each other and to the site, and melding gardens into a natural landscape that was itself already rich in beauty and diversity, *above* and *below*.

Ideas of aligning the garden with lifestyle took hold. John Brookes was an early proponent of this style of garden making. In his 1969 book, *The Room Outside,* and in his own garden at Denmans in Sussex, England, *right* and *opposite*, he supported his work with practice, advocating for color, comfort and convenience, not just in plants, but also in furnishing and plan.

National and international postwar festivals were game-changers. The Festival of Britain in 1951 was staged to advance—and revive—industry and the sciences, a worthy testament to the future vitality of a country—and world—emerging from war. One part of the festival, The Pleasure Gardens, was devoted entirely to recreation and fun. The cover of the guidebook, *right,* gives a hint of the attractions to be found. Situated in Battersea Park, it harked back to the pleasure gardens of the eighteenth and early nineteenth centuries, like Vauxhall

and Ranelagh, the most popular among many that were dotted around London. Music, food, and theater were on the menu, and the beer gardens were named after individual pleasure gardens. In design, too, the gardens looked back rather than forward, and featured a petting zoo and Punch and Judy theatre for children, fairground rides imported from the USA, a dance pavilion in the form of a circus big top, and many shops vending goods from all over the world.

In Europe, it was a different story. In England particularly, midcentury modern outdoor living spaces retained the "plantcentricity" that was a part of the culture (you could think there is a specific gene in the British code for it), but at the same time they became more relaxed—less of a token landscape tableau and more of a self-portrait, as a statement created to reveal tastes and interests. Formality was pushed to one side, while the lushness that was so easy to cultivate in a mild, even climate was given plenty of space to work its magic.

While the first section of this book broadly describes how we arrived at midcentury modern style, this second section considers the legacy of that design period, and how garden designers and landscape architects are expressing it today.

A good many paragraphs have been written about the midcentury modern aesthetic, but these usually center on architecture and interior design. In fact, researching archive illustrations for this book was limited by this fact, as photography predominantly focused on the buildings, and very rarely did the photographer pull back far enough to show the house in its natural setting, or to hint at what the garden might have looked like. This is less true today, certainly, but our quandary has been how to show the midcentury modern ethos that underpinned the architecture and landscaping of the period, one that put humanity's needs and aspirations at the center of the plan.

WHAT MADE THE PERIOD'S STYLE SO ATTRACTIVE... WAS ITS EMBRACE OF INDIVIDUALITY

Archive photographs often include people in the frame, clearly demonstrating that entertainment in the home was a key part of the lifestyle—guests arriving for cocktail hour step through the atrium, heading for the terrace where the hosts greet them with canapés and martinis. By comparison, today's photographs, of both interior and exterior, are most often devoid of human life, and the gardens, created for outdoor living, are really just artifacts—people would simply clutter up the view. There is a reverent sterility to the pictures, and it's particularly apparent in the way midcentury modern properties are shown, as though the Eichler, May, Wexler, Neutra and others' houses were museum displays, carefully "curated" in restoration. Where is the humanity that led to their creation? Lost in the curation, as new owners overdo nostalgia and mistake imposing internal views unimpeded by walls for "being true to the original vision." Just as there were magazines in the 1950s that were guides to modern living, today there are magazines devoted to midcentury modern style larded with advertisements for retro-repro. So you *can* have a period-style, turquoise throw rug to give a "pop of color" to the pristine white interior of your free-flowing open plan midcentury modern ranch.

This seems to be missing the point of what made the period's style so attractive, and that was its embrace of individuality. The house may have been part of a tract development, and the street frontage exterior as bland and unassuming as its neighbor's, but

The idea of an inseparable connection between house and garden was central to midcentury modern design, but so was the notion that people were similarly integrated with their homes. Part of transparent living was being able to see what the kids were up to in the garden or the playroom, and ensuring that food preparation and dining happened in the same space. Enabling the easy flow of life was paramount to being modern.

Homes designed by Eliot Noyes (see page 38) captured the zeitgeist, and on the porch of a summerhouse he designed for the Rantoul family, *opposite,* cocktail hour is in progress, and the table is set for dinner al fresco. "Outdoor living is fun" was the message, and it was expressed in many ways. From a simple picnic spread a few feet from the porch, *below,* an abstract-shaped swimming pool, *left,* or the simplicity of an atrium revived by a few free-form furnishing pieces, *above.*

Authentic midcentury modern interiors and landscapes were typically richly textured and deeply personalized spaces. Midcentury design icons Charles and Ray Eames, pictured *opposite* in the living room of Case Study House #8 that Charles himself designed, layered ethnic knick-knacks with craftsman-made ceramics, multi-patterned hand-woven textiles, Japanese paper lanterns and silver candlesticks to warm and enliven a super-modern interior.

Avoid the anodyne: mixing shapes, patterns and materials gives personality to a room, indoors or out. The ever-popular Bertoia wire frame occasional chair and tulip table are classics, but to avoid the "carefully curated" look, spread out a tribal textile like a Navajo blanket, stir in some wood, raw stone and metal surfaces, and the result is personal *and* expressive of the warmth and vitality of midcentury modern design.

the interior—and the exterior living area behind the house (aka garden)—could have been a lively mix of stylish modern pieces and collections of folk and ethnic art, Persian carpets, hand-woven textiles and craftsman-made tabletop pieces. Look closely at the interior of Ray and Charles Eames own home; African carvings, Japanese lanterns and ethnic rugs dilute the stark modernity of the Eames furnishings, transforming their living space into a comfortable, entertaining interior. Cliff May, too, had an opinion on the value of the handmade versus the mass-produced: "Nowadays the collectors are always going for the perfect rug. But in architecture we try to make our architecture not perfect. I mean, we like to have it asymmetrical, and, if we have a little wave

or bump in the eave line, we like it better, and if the plaster is put on carelessly and randomly so it doesn't look machine made. You take a Navajo rug that looks like it's been made by a machine, why, it doesn't have handcrafted value. To me, I would value the handmade so much more than I would machine made."

Outdoors, this would translate into a lively interplay of textures and colors between hardscaping materials, pieces of outdoor art (even Picasso made ceramic sculpture for outdoor use) and signature plants. The organic shapes of furnishings like Bertoia's wire frame butterfly chairs further defined the outdoor décor. The garden was inviting, entertaining, and lived in. And, just like the interior, an expression of the homeowner's personality.

Authentic midcentury modern interiors and landscapes were typically richly textured and deeply personalized spaces. Midcentury design icons Charles and Ray Eames, pictured *opposite* in the living room of Case Study House #8 that Charles himself designed, layered ethnic knick-knacks with craftsman-made ceramics, multi-patterned hand-woven textiles, Japanese paper lanterns and silver candlesticks to warm and enliven a super-modern interior.

Avoid the anodyne: mixing shapes, patterns and materials gives personality to a room, indoors or out. The ever-popular Bertoia wire frame occasional chair and tulip table are classics, but to avoid the "carefully curated" look, spread out a tribal textile like a Navajo blanket, stir in some wood, raw stone and metal surfaces, and the result is personal *and* expressive of the warmth and vitality of midcentury modern design.

the interior—and the exterior living area behind the house (aka garden)—could have been a lively mix of stylish modern pieces and collections of folk and ethnic art, Persian carpets, hand-woven textiles and craftsman-made tabletop pieces. Look closely at the interior of Ray and Charles Eames own home; African carvings, Japanese lanterns and ethnic rugs dilute the stark modernity of the Eames furnishings, transforming their living space into a comfortable, entertaining interior. Cliff May, too, had an opinion on the value of the handmade versus the mass-produced: "Nowadays the collectors are always going for the perfect rug. But in architecture we try to make our architecture not perfect. I mean, we like to have it asymmetrical, and, if we have a little wave or bump in the eave line, we like it better, and if the plaster is put on carelessly and randomly so it doesn't look machine made. You take a Navajo rug that looks like it's been made by a machine, why, it doesn't have handcrafted value. To me, I would value the handmade so much more than I would machine made."

Outdoors, this would translate into a lively interplay of textures and colors between hardscaping materials, pieces of outdoor art (even Picasso made ceramic sculpture for outdoor use) and signature plants. The organic shapes of furnishings like Bertoia's wire frame butterfly chairs further defined the outdoor décor. The garden was inviting, entertaining, and lived in. And, just like the interior, an expression of the homeowner's personality.

INSIDE STORY THE LEGACY OF MCM LANDSCAPING

"Core values" is a widely used term, one that embodies Monterey, California- based landscape architect Bernard Trainor's design philosophy. "Successful design in architecture is type driven, responding well to its location." In this case, in the courtyard of a midcentury modern home, Trainor shaped a place suited either to companionable entertaining or the simple act of sitting quietly alone.

Originally from Australia, Trainor's early influences were architects Glen Murcutt and Robin Boyd, but during a lengthy stay in England, Trainor sought out Beth Chatto. He lived and worked in her garden, and from her learned "to observe the place you're in to find the solution to a planting scheme. Beth was a catalyst; she celebrated place allied to having a realistic point of view about what would work."

In the garden shown here, rich textures in hardscape and furnishings accent the strong, low, horizontal sweep of the roofline, and pops of color from painted surfaces and flowers enhance the cool green surrounds. The plants introduce the vertical element, thereby keeping the space engaging; a hedge of *Anigozanthos* (kangaroo paw) defines the social area centered on a low, stone firepit.

Trainor's planting combines what he terms regional planting and plant "counterparts"—plants that are not native, but which thrive in similar conditions in other parts of the world. Given California's dry summers and mild, wet winters, Mediterranean and southern hemisphere plants offer a broad plant palette to create an all-important sense of place.

INSIDE STORY
BREAKING DOWN BARRIERS

"When you can't go out, go up" could be the design brief for this postage stamp garden carved out of the extension behind a period house in an historic neighborhood in Melbourne, Australia.

Starting with a late Victorian workingman's cottage, local architect Matt Gibson designed the renovation to conserve the vintage façade's lacey ironwork frill that frames the porch, and to preserve the period brick and board construction. Taking inspiration from the work of modernist architect Mies van der Rohe, the extension at the back of the old house occupies most of the long narrow garden space, transforming the property into a modern space where indoors and outdoors merge perfectly in true midcentury fashion.

The construction—true to modernist ideals—lacks ornament, but makes up for it in the ingenious use of limited space. Opening off the dining/kitchen area, a small courtyard garden is lush with foliage plants—a green oasis visible from the farthest end of the ground floor. On the other side of the courtyard's brick wall is a swimming pool and recreation area.

Called "Abstract House," the design scheme references the midcentury modern accent on form, line, and most importantly, flow. Glass walls slide away, removing even the most tenuous division between the outdoors and the indoors. And yet this is the most intimate floor of the house, where bedrooms, bathrooms and family-centered rooms are located.

Midcentury modern landscape and architecture is united by its diversity in form, shape, color, and texture. Ernest Braun— a key photographer of the period— perfectly captured this reliance on contrasts in design in the image *opposite*. The snaking branches of a tree, its roots carefully conserved in a planting well, accent the linear architecture. Thomas Church thought a single tree, well formed, was the most valuable element in a landscape plan.

All gardens have perimeter walls of some sort, and furnishings; add saturated color to intensify light and shadow and the commonplace becomes art.

CONTRASTS IN DESIGN

The Architecture of Humanism by Englishman Geoffrey Scott was first published on the eve of the First World War and sank without trace, only to be republished in 1924 and lauded by the likes of Edith Wharton (novelist and author of *The Decoration of Houses*). Seventy years later, Geoffrey Jellicoe described to me how the book had turned architectural thinking on its head. As if to testify to the truth of this, Denys Lasdun, the English architect of London's Royal National Theatre and the University of East Anglia, (the latter landscaped by Brenda Colvin, as described on page 53) said in an interview that its focus on understanding that architecture is really about modeling space had a significant impact on his work and that of other midcentury modernists.

Lao-Tse, the legendary sixth-century Chinese scholar and founder of Taoism, said it first: "The reality of the building does not consist in roof and walls, but in the space within to be lived in." The idea that space was what shaped a building, and that the way we lived within dictated the space may not have been strictly speaking about architectural space, but about inner space, where life happens; within cell walls, between grains of sand, within our hearts. But, in our gardens and our homes, how we enhance that inner space, with color, texture, and forms, is what shapes its character while expressing who we are.

Scott planned to follow his polemic with a book about taste, but got no further than the opening line, "It is very difficult…" Truer words

IN THE CASE OF MIDCENTURY
MODERN DESIGN, CONTRAST
WAS THE DESIGN DYNAMIC—
A RESPONSE TO THE ENERGY
THAT WAS FUELLED BY PEOPLE'S
HOPE FOR A BRIGHT FUTURE

about design have never been written. Ultimately, taste is culturally subjective, and this is especially true when it comes to garden design, as was expressed by Geoffrey Jellicoe when he said, "The private garden remains constant as the peculiar expression of the individual." And in the case of midcentury modern design, contrast was the design dynamic—a response to the energy that was fuelled by people's hope for a bright future.

The color element
Color is surely the most subjective element in design, and today white—the absence of color—seems to be the popular choice. Does this reflect the contemporary wish for simplicity in lifestyles that

we are seeking and finding in midcentury modern design, or is it just the easy way out? A time-traveler from the 1950s would probably be aghast to see such a visual void, and marvel at our acceptance of bland neutrality. In the period, color and its close allies, texture and shape, were bursting out all over in unexpected ways—just another expression of the optimism of the period.

As an art student at the tail end of the 1960s, I was given the textbook *The Enjoyment and Use of Color* by Walter Sargent. It was a 1964 paperback of the original, first published in 1923 by Scribners. It remains one of the most influential books on color theory for artists, another being *Interactions of Color* by Josef Albers, who, along with his wife Anni, was a key figure in the modernist movement.

Opposite, the garden of the Villa Noailles in Hyères, France was designed by Robert Mallet Stevens in the early 1920s for the Vicomte de Noailles and his wife, who were patrons of surrealist artists including Salvador Dali and Jean Cocteau. Built of reinforced concrete, the square grid and angular walls hint at the concealed construction in good modernist style, and the planting serves predominantly to enhance the pictorial element.

Thinking of the hardscape and architecture as part of the design plane, with each given its own surface character, has given purpose to the entrance to the Australian house *above*. The color red advances in our field of vision and draws us towards it; its use at the entryway serves as an invitation to "come on in."

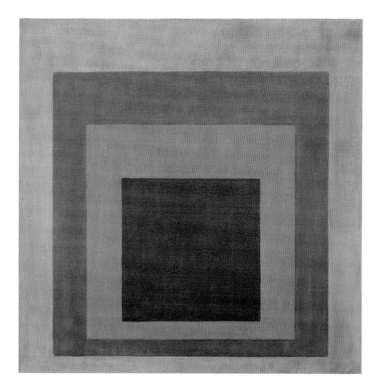 

Color was enormously important to midcentury modern designers, and the theory work of Josef Albers paved the way for new methods of color distribution in the home. His experiments resulted in a series of paintings, "Homage to a Square," including the two *above* executed in 1968 (*left*) and 1954 (*right*).

Frank Lloyd Wright's color palette for his Taliesin homes inspired commercial paint manufacturers to develop a similar range of paints (including his favorite "Cherokee Red"), *opposite*; other manufacturers followed suit, like Dunn Edwards in California, who developed an Eichler color palette.

Albers was a Bauhaus Master and its assistant director under Mies van der Rohe until its closure in 1933, after which he accepted an offer from Philip Johnson to teach at the Black Mountain School. His work on color theory continued there and was formalized in the class he taught on color—he was, by all accounts, an inspiring and innovative instructor. He did not teach art, he said, but seeing. He taught that simplicity was a social obligation and great design was simple, and that "there are no fine or applied arts, only good or bad art." All were tenets that struck a chord with midcentury architects and landscapers.

Yale University, where Albers later taught, published the original edition of his book; it was a boxed collection of silkscreen printed color sheets—examples of his experiments with color—and two thin booklets. It was beyond my reach and that of most students of the time, but my teachers adopted Albers' methods of hands-on experiment using Color-Aid paper. It was a delicious collection of silk-screen printed paper sheets, six inches by nine inches, which we cut and tore into strips and random shapes to create our own experience of color. I have those papers today and still enjoy experimenting with the effects that can be achieved juxtaposing and coordinating the tints and hues of one or several sheets. It did indeed teach me to see.

Interaction of Color became available in an affordable paperback in the 1970s, and in 2013, to celebrate the 50th

TALIESIN PALETTE IN MARTIN-SENOUR PAINTS

anniversary of the book's publication, Yale issued an interactive app for digital devices to insure its relevance to future generations. With over 125 color studies and interactive plates that replicate working with paper, you can manipulate colors and combinations to your heart's content. And at the same time get a glimpse into the fascinated minds of midcentury modern designers as they learned that color was so much more than surface treatment; that it could express mood and intention, and affect our emotional responses.

Which brings us back to the post-war high spirits of the period. In keeping with a desire by architects to settle a house into its natural surroundings, their exterior colors were often neutral or earthy; paint companies created Taliesin color ways to get the southwest Frank Lloyd Wright look; Dunn Edwards produced a range of exterior paints and stains for Eichler houses that ranged from deep forest green to buff sandstone in hue. The bouncy bright jelly bean colors—glossy pink, scarlet red, mint green, aquamarine and turquoise—all had their place in midcentury decorative themes, mainly in the interior, but often in the garden too. Plastic laminate garden chairs, parasols, awnings, cushion covers, table settings, and placemats were all given the bright touch, contrasting completely with the reserved, low-key exterior. Color was used to express a personal statement: "Yes, publicly I conform to the norm, but internally, I'm a bold individualist."

The florid patterns of Josef Frank's textile designs that he developed for Svenskt Tenn, the Swedish interior design company, include "Primavera," *left,* "Mirakel," designed in the 1920s, *opposite above,* and "Terrazzo," *opposite below,* from 1944. This last one is different from Frank's output as it represents an inorganic motif, inspired by the terrazzo flooring material that was becoming so popular in midcentury modern interior design. Formed from chips of marble or granite embedded in concrete, it was extremely durable, and if crushed oyster shell, glass chips or other suitable, shiny materials were included, added a lively contrast to interior surfaces. It was one of Richard Neutra's specified flooring treatments.

Estrid Ericson started the department store Svenskt Tenn; she is seen *above* with Josef Frank on the shop floor. Through their design partnership, the Swedish influence on European midcentury modernism was consolidated.

Josef Frank: The fabric of modernism

"It doesn't matter if you mix old and new, or different styles, colors and patterns. The things you like will always blend, by themselves, into a peaceful whole." So said Austrian architect Josef Frank in 1958, explaining in part his theory of "accidentism." This could be interpreted to suggest that things that belong together will find each other; an idea for which Frank is arguably living proof. Fleeing the rise of fascism in 1933, Frank left his native Austria for exile in Sweden—a move which would come to define his career.

As a founding member of the Austrian Werkbund, a collaborative of progressive designers, and the Austrian Union of Settlers and Small Gardeners, which sought to improve everyday life for common working families, Frank had little liking for the house-as-machine diktat of Le Corbusier, and the hard-edge design and spare uniformity of Walter Gropius, the Bauhaus and fellow modernists. He regarded their doctrine as dangerously elitist.

Frank believed in the simple functions of living, at base that "the house is not a work of art, simply a place where one lives." While externally his architecture had something in common with Corbusier's bland white modernist boxes, internally their styles could not have been more different. Frank was careful to make the most of natural light to illuminate the interiors, and to create little social islands where families could eat, work, and play. Most of all he kept his design focus on making the home a happy place to live.

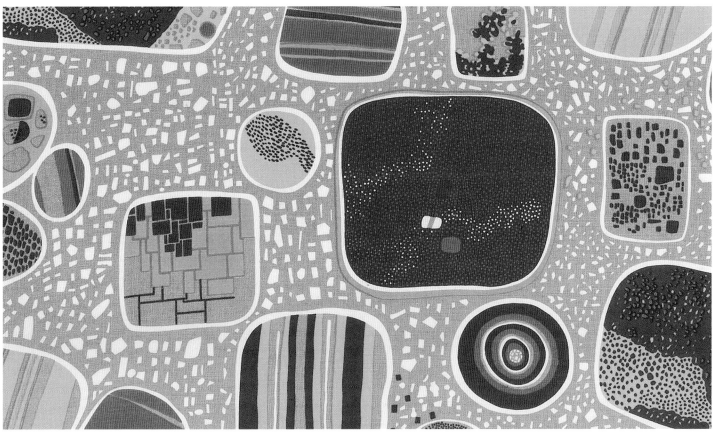

Frank's wit and vision is best seen in his work for the Swedish company Svenskt Tenn. On arriving in Stockholm, Frank was brought into the company by its founder, Estrid Ericson. An art teacher, Ericson was inspired by the philosophy of William Morris and the English Arts and Crafts movement, and in 1924 she opened a store dedicated to selling handcrafted decorative items made almost exclusively by Swedish designers and crafts workshops. By the 1930s, the store had gained recognition as the most important design house in Scandinavia. Amid his myriad textile and architectural drawings for Svenskt Tenn, Frank produced more than 2,000 furniture designs. One of his earliest was for a sofa that was 140 centimeters deep and covered in one

of his signature exotic-print fabrics. The norm at the time was eighty centimeters, and so his design was ridiculed by some as an outrageous extravaganza of over-stuffed upholstery. Such voluptuous pieces were, however, an immediate success with designers. Frank believed that clients wanted comfort and gaiety in their homes, and providing that was his forté. His textile designs in particular made both his and Svenskt Tenn's names, and what is particularly attractive about these fabrics— aside from their vivid hues and super-size repeats—is the way the exaggerated nature motifs, bearing names such as "Brazil," "Italian Dinner," "Hawaii" and "Terrazzo," bring the warmth of sunnier climes into the home. Something particularly appreciated by northern countries

"The house," said Josef Frank, "is not a work of art, simply a place where one lives." Yet living can be done artfully, with a mind to satisfy the senses. The contemporary Svenskt Tenn showroom, *opposite*, touches all visual and tactile senses, while the garden rooms *above* and *right* speak to other sensory delights. In particular, the soothing sounds of grasses whispering in the breeze, the cooling visual effect of water rippling over stones, and the satisfying Zen-like serenity of seclusion.

like Sweden, whose summer's are fleeting and daylight hours extremely limited during winter months.

Frank and Ericson took eclecticism to new heights, bringing together (in a seemingly random order) art pieces, wildly differing patterns, colors and textures, and antique and ethnic furnishings in a heady mix of contrasts. Frank recognized that people wanted to take pleasure in their homes and gardens, and therefore, in contrast to hard-core modernists, was a friend to ornament. In that respect, he can be said to have paved the way for the simple light-hearted functionalism of Swedish design. This is a lasting influence that can be seen in the designs of Habitat and Marimekko during the 1960s and in Ikea today, and one that, crucially, works both inside and out.

Nevertheless, this attitude to ornament may not have always produced design that was in good taste, particularly if it was not kept in balance. As Garrett Eckbo described in his book, *Home Landscaping* (which as mentioned earlier, was an expert guide, perhaps *the* guide, to midcentury modern landscaping) a room and garden needed to have the right kind of *enriching elements*—"not so much as to be cluttered, not so few as to seem barren."

Living color

Traditional Japanese gardens were a popular influence on midcentury modern garden design, not only because of their apparent simplicity and discreet use of ornamentation, but

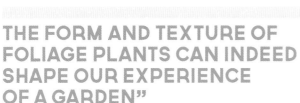

Gilles Clément took advantage of this when designing the public gardens in Paris known as Parc André-Citroën, *right* and *above*. On the 35-acre site of the old Citroën car works, Clément developed a park with a series of internal garden areas, each representing colors of the alchemical metals (gold, lead, mercury, etc.), their associated planets and senses, as well as the various physical conditions associated with water, from wet to arid. In another area of the park, the grasses grown were selected for the way they moved in the wind, and there are "entertainment" elements throughout, including a fountain controlled by a computer.

Opposite, a garden design by Garrett Eckbo in the 1950s references the cubist garden of the Villa Noailles (see page 100). One can only marvel at the upkeep such a strenuous plan would entail. Eckbo had ambitious ideas, sometimes at odds with the concept of easy living.

THE FORM AND TEXTURE OF FOLIAGE PLANTS CAN INDEED SHAPE OUR EXPERIENCE OF A GARDEN"

because of their minimal use of flower color for impact. Instead, they took advantage of the many varied tints of green found throughout nature—from the silver blues and grays found most widely in arid climates, to the luxuriant inky emerald greens of foliage plants. Add to this the myriad shapes and textures of trees, shrubs and evergreens and the garden scene is at once tranquil and lively. The form and texture of foliage plants can indeed shape our experience of a garden—soft mounds of silvery felted leaves fade into the background and soothe us, while jagged, prickly spikes capture the attention and make us jumpy (and cautious!)

But combine the two and the planting takes on a personality all of its own. Add dabs of flower color and you have art. Whether you are making a garden from scratch on a site scraped bare by the developer or working within a natural landscape, with a stunning view or even just one good tree, paint the garden picture with restraint.

Texture enhancements

Eckbo hit on something when he presented the elements of décor as enrichment, and related the way they are used to the way an interior is organized, which is essentially the same, but simpler. A chair is a chair, inside or out, but for outdoor use, he advised a streamlined, uncluttered shape, yet one that is nonetheless inviting; living room fireplaces encourage conviviality, and

outdoors a simple patio firepit, perhaps one reminiscent of Jens Jensen's council ring configurations, signals a gathering place. Eckbo recognized that the variety of enrichments were many, from the natural—plants in the ground to pools of water, rocks, driftwood, which he categorized as "found art"—to the man-made—furniture, screening, sculpture or other objects of art (which he quaintly acknowledges are generally rarely found, "because of the poverty-stricken character of most of those available to the average pocketbook.")

Hardscape surface textures in a midcentury modern garden are more dominant than the texture provided by plant foliage and stems. However, the contrasts made by dancing shadows of plants cast against smooth stuccoed walls or across broad sweeps of paving add an incomparable texture and movement; the semi-transparency of trellis work and lattice screen can complement the translucence of acrylic polycarbonate sheeting used as fencing panels. Reflections bouncing off swimming pools and ornamental water features contrast the sheen of glass patio doors or tabletops. Textured fabrics could be contrasted against smooth plastic furniture; delicate wire-framed furniture can be paired with a granite-topped table on a sturdy wooden base. These simple effects of contrast, deployed in moderation, will fill an outdoor space with character.

Palm Springs architect William Krisel designed a style of house where the roofline took flight from the ridge beam, allowing clerestory lights under the eaves. So-called "Butterfly Houses" became his signature, and as he was most involved in developing tract housing, there are quite a few around. The house *opposite* is based on Krisel's design, but has an equally distinctive garden: a geometric pattern of various colored granites framing circles of faux grass.

Midcentury modern homes may have been characterized by right angles, but in contrast, landscapes were often filled with curves, *above* and *right*.

Enhancing shape

If there is a shape that is emblematic of midcentury modern landscape design it has to be the chubby boomerang-cum-kidney shape: this could be found in swimming pools, occasional tables, butterfly chairs, flowerbeds, textile motifs. It was everywhere in the postwar period. For décor, curves were preferred to straight lines and sharp angles, which may have had something to do with notions of comfortable informality in the new age of easy living.

Shape in garden design is typically thought of in terms of plant outlines—the rounded crowns of deciduous trees, the low fan-shaped spread of shrubs, the upright thrusting spikes of evergreens, the amorphous froth of massed perennials, and so on. But shape can also describe space in the garden as defined by the ebb and flow of smooth paving paired with coarsely textured gravel, the perspective lines described in space by pergola beams or the confined spaces shaped by fencing. So how the space is molded depends on how it is "drawn" by structural details. Do fences have to be linear constructs? Screens can be curved around the space they are defining rather than set as squares or rectangles to form walls. The landing pad effect of flat swathes of concrete block paving can be relieved by carpets of pebble mosaic, the edges nibbled away by mats of groundcovering plants.

And don't forget light and shade; areas of each will further shape how a space is used. In fact, the most significant element

Curves were most generously put to use in the design of swimming pools—for even the most rectangular of lots, *opposite* and *above*. This is a design trope that has largely been ignored as lap pools and negative edges take over from contouring to enhance a site. Yet curves are the most organic form in nature; looking at outdoor furniture today it is mostly angular but the curvaceous was once the mode, and deck furniture conformed to the shape of the human body at rest, *right*.

of shaping space in the style of a midcentury modern garden will come at the point where indoors meets the outdoors. Shading this transition point with a pergola or ramada will ease their integration, and support the perception that the garden is made for outdoor living.

Art embellishments: I know what I like
Of all the man-made enhancements that go into garden making, none depends more on questions of taste than the "what and how" of including an art piece in the garden. Eckbo was only partly right in observing that the quality depends on the size of the pocketbook. We've all seen art that costs millions but for which we wouldn't give

two pennies. Some think there is nothing more beautiful than a well-made bottle tree, others are happy with a chainsaw-sculpted grizzly bear. The border between garden art and yard art is a fuzzy one, and in either case a good rule of thumb to follow is to use it sparingly, and do so with conviction in the sure knowledge that the piece is something you love. This is a rule of thumb that I recommend you apply to all your design choices:

"Have nothing in your houses that you do not know to be useful, or believe to be beautiful."

William Morris, *The Beauty of Life*, 1880.

INSIDE STORY
DEFINING SPACE WITH COLOR

The late Mexican architect Luis Barragán famously countered the midcentury veneration of plate glass by saying, "All architecture that does not express serenity falls In Its spiritual mission. Thus, it has been a mistake to abandon the shelter of walls for the inclemency of large areas of glass." And certainly, in the crystalline light of the Southwest, where dense shadows cut like knives across the view and color is seen at its most saturated, too many glittering expanses of glass can only be a distraction.

Color, however, is another matter. Barragán took the white-cube austerity of International Style modernism and translated it into richly colored and textured structures, developing a distinct language of Mexican modernism, one that references the vernacular architecture of the land and clarity of the light there. This new vernacular can be seen throughout Caudra San Cristóba, *opposite*, an equestrian estate built in 1968 near Mexico City. The visual and spatial values of numerous jewel-colored stucco walls reflected in its many pools of water have been adapted to landscapes everywhere, but especially in the American Southwest.

"The power of walls to shape a garden cannot be underestimated," says Steve Martino, a landscape designer and sculptor based in Phoenix, Arizona. The sculptural advantage of a good wall in a rich color seen in bright desert light is something Martino exploits in many of his projects. An award-winning garden in Phoenix, *right*, and a more recent Palm Springs garden, *below*, show what he means by "design is all about edges, and how one material meets another."

INSIDE STORY 2D ABSTRACTION IN 3D LANDSCAPES

For a property in Florida that followed modernist architecture's mode of inflexible white geometry, *below* and *opposite below*, Raymond Jungles designed a luxuriant landscape that is an intoxicating blend of polished marble and concrete hardscaping, coupled with sensuous plant shapes and scintillating color that only be found in tropical flora.

Since that project, Jungles' oeuvre has spread to public landscaping projects, including a major condo development in the historic Coconut Grove, Florida. But residential work remains his forte, and he brings to planting design some of the painterly qualities he learned from his mentor, the renowned midcentury Brazilian painter and landscape designer Roberto Burle Marx, with whom Jungles worked intermittently over the course of more than a decade.

Burle Marx trained as a fine artist in Europe, and as a young man came to South America in the Jewish diaspora. He soon embraced the native plants of the Amazon as his artistic muse. From his studio in Rio de Janeiro, *left*, came paintings that inspired his designs for tapestry, mosaic, jewelry, and of course, landscapes, including his own garden, *opposite above*. Now the Sítio Roberto Burle Marx, it remains a treasure trove of South American tropicals—some 3,500 species—many of which he personally collected and subsequently introduced to popular cultivation. For Jungles, Marx's legacy is the knowledge that gardens are for living; a place to celebrate the goodness of life and the joys of friendship, and where artistic expression engages all the senses.

One can take a bold approach to the design of a housing landscape, or the actual approach to a house can be bold. In the realm of the former, Chicago-based landscape architecture firm Hoerr Shaudt's commission for a north Michigan summerhouse, *opposite,* called for a tranquil domestic oasis with an Asian influence that would coexist with the energetic native landscape. Strong blocks of groundcover and generous sweeps of native grasses spread below a grove of trees set the perfect tone for the restrained architecture.

Today, the "approach" to a house most often means a broad sweep of driveway terminating at a double or even three-car garage door, *right,* facing blindly onto the street. The house entrance is insignificant by comparison. The balance is off. However, single-car garages were the norm for midcentury modern homes, and as at this Quincy Jones house, *above,* the scale did not overwhelm a recessed front door.

BOLD APPROACHES

Today's focus on "curb appeal" is in direct opposition to how the authentic midcentury modern house presented its face to the world, which could be described as modestly, even discreetly. This despite the soaring ridge lines and bold angularity marking the midcentury architectural idea, projecting the boldness and optimism that lay at the heart of the period.

Many larger houses built within the past few decades have ostentatious porticoed entries that overwhelm the front entrance porch, and which bear little relationship to the scale of the house. Such a treatment would be intimidating to an approaching visitor if it weren't so outlandish (at best they distract from the mundane design of the buildings they front). Midcentury modern homes,

on the other hand, took trouble to downplay the actual entrance, setting the door into a recessed front porch so that the playful sophistication of the architecture is not obscured.

Pierced brick screens or offset fences often further disguised the front entrance, although not the elevations of the house and its surrounding landscape; the idea was to keep the approach in "scale" with the house, its environment, and the people using it. Tommy Church, writing about the importance of balancing scale when designing a garden in *Gardens are for People,* advised, "The best rule to follow is: when in doubt, make it larger. The eye detects a meager dimension more easily than it does a too-generous one." The generosity he's advocating, however, comes not in terms of

For all their sweeping rooflines, plate-glass walls and futuristic detailing, many midcentury homes had low-key entrances. Some were so carefully blended into the exterior façades, that were it not for dramatic plant groupings, *opposite*, or bright colors, *below*, it would be hard to identify them. Paving, too, expressed the way in, *above*, and see-through partitions hinted at the private garden beyond, *left*.

The Kauffman House by legendary midcentury modern architect Richard Neutra, *above, left,* and *on the cover*, is a lesson in discretion. The bunker-like effect of the structure rising behind a native boulder-strewn landscape screens the private part of the house and the extensive views of the desert.

The Brick Weave House in Chicago, *opposite,* is the architectural firm Studio Gang's bold answer to providing privacy to a townhouse—one of a densely built row that is separated from the roadway and sidewalk by just a few feet. Brickweave screening, enclosing even the tiniest front yards, is traditional in the Middle East and Southeast Asia, enlivening the streetscape, while adding a rich shadow play to the home's interior.

"A TREE, PLACED TO FRAME THE HOUSE OR CAST ITS SHADOW ON IT, DOES MORE SOFTENING THAN A FOREST OF SHRUBS"

making a triumphal entrance, but in creating, for example, an ample approach rather than a narrow linear path leading to the front door. One of the ways midcentury modern designers expressed this was by using broad rectangular pavers of stone or poured concrete laid in a staggered path toward the entrance area.

Plantings were accents; trees were used sparingly as specimens or anchors to "hold" the scheme to its site: "A tree, placed to frame the house or cast its shadow on it, does more softening than a forest of shrubs" wrote Church. He favored this arrangement over foundation planting, "an unsightly excess of padding of overgrown bushes and trees" that blocked out natural light and through which visitors had to "grope" their way to the front door.

Understatement was the byword for perfection. Taking inspiration from the clean lines of the architecture itself, hardscaping was pared down and uncluttered. By using native stone, natural materials and site-appropriate plants, the front garden areas signaled to visitors that the house had been woven into its site, reflecting Frank Lloyd Wright's belief that a building should be "one with the land" and not simply plopped down on top of it.

One of the other defining characteristics of midcentury modern architecture was the emphasis placed on the external features of a design; a house was meant to function as more than a shelter, and in some instances was elevated by its design to a multi-dimensional artistic statement. This is most obviously expressed in the front

Rethink steps. Low-risers and broad treads make the climb from path to door easier, particularly for the elderly and those not sure of the their footing. From a design perspective, such configurations are well suited to extending the garden terrace or signaling a change in mood or direction in the landscape.

Staggered platforms rising through the garden, *above*, slow the pace, and steps offset to run at right angles to the house, *opposite*, make it a journey from street to door. Working with the natural ground contours can dictate a natural stair run, *left,* and where steps are lacking, *below*, a heavy metal panel on a pivot hinge makes a dramatic entrance .

Deep overhangs and delicate supports make for elegant terraces, particularly when interior flooring can be carried through to the outdoor spaces, or where floor-to-ceiling glass partitions are used, as in the designs *on this page.* Built-in storage can run the length of the wall indoors and out, as it does in the home in Melbourne, Australia, *opposite.*

elevation. Instead of opting for the traditional triangular-based or craftsman style roof lines, midcentury modern homes might have multiple roof lines at different levels, showing off the complexity of the overall design and the uncommon silhouette of the structure. Horizontal lines, elongated vaulted ceilings, and dramatic overhangs could be extended over terraces and used as carports. Building materials and color palettes were selected to help blend the structure into the site as it stretched into the garden. Far from being add-ons or appearing as afterthoughts, these constructions contributed to the strong, unified, midcentury modern silhouette that is instantly recognizable, blending in color and texture yet contrasting in line and form with the surrounding landscape. And as the lines and

building materials of the house integrate with the materials used outdoors, we see the use of outdoor paving spreading across the threshold and into not only the high-traffic areas of the house, but into recreational areas, making living rooms and patios one contiguous unit.

Another ideal for the time was for new homes to feel more organically connected to the landscape, and a deck or platform was the perfect answer to extending living outdoors. Sweeping lawns front and back were one option, but their high maintenance and demands on summer water supply made them impractical. Hardscaping materials such as concrete pavers were used to extend the architectural lines of the house to make a seamless boundary

Boulders or a specimen tree are visual anchors on broad terraces, *above* and *left*. Pay attention, too, to the lighting; illuminate path edging, but save the brightest lighting for the entranceway to provide a warm welcome, *opposite.*

HARDSCAPING MATERIALS SUCH AS CONCRETE PAVERS WERE USED TO EXTEND THE ARCHITECTURAL LINES OF THE HOUSE

between indoors and outside. Cliff May's tract-built houses displayed a frontage sheltered by a long ramada; for modest midcentury modern houses the only element of public display was the car parking area. Often set at a right angle to the front door, it was an integral part of the layout. But by the 1970s, in tract-built suburbia, architecture had left the room and construction took over. The garage-in-front layout developed and the actual housefront was given little thought: if you didn't notice it, did it matter what it looked like?

Today's garden space is often at a premium; zero-lot line plotting means there is little or no frontage to work with, and in crowded urban areas, what front garden there is has often been transformed into concrete pads for off-street parking. If there is garden space,

the challenge is making the area seem larger than it is. The blurring of indoors and outdoors with glass walls that can be opened wide when weather permits is the obvious and popular solution, but breaking up the garden space into hidden corners, or meandering paths that keep the eye entertained as it takes in the view, will give an impression of space. "The eye," as Church described it, "prefers to move around a garden on lines that are provocative, never lose their interest, never end in dead corners, occasionally provide excitement or surprise, and always leave you interested and contented." Thus, a recessed entry into the garden, tucked into the shadows or screened by brick tracery walls, will lure you into the garden beyond, where the activities of life are enjoyed in the company of family and friends.

Never miss an opportunity for bold, native planting at an entrance. *Left*, the entrance to a tropical garden in Miami, clothed in evergreens, fan palms and bananas, all underplanted with bromeliads and ferns, is a voyage of discovery to the front door. *Above*, a stone staircase makes a precipitous climb through a hillside garden. *Below*, varied evergreens contrast perfectly with the bright red frontage and hard architectural lines of an Australian home.

Opposite above, the desert pushes up against the entrance of a Palm Springs house. *Opposite below*, an exotic composition of plant forms and textures is juxtaposed with rough-hewn screening walls and block paving on the approach to a villa in Monterrey, Mexico.

Opposite, a steep flight of polished stone steps is broken with shallow landings, the better to help climbers catch their breath.

Matt Gibson's design for the Concrete House in Melbourne, *above*, took advantage of a deep frontage to shape a sweeping entry court; a counterpoint to the complex interior spaces that move from open to closed, and public to private.

Above, the uneven edge of the interior floor creeps outdoors beyond the sliding glass; the broken line is a playful transition between inside and out.

In a hillside landscape near Carmel, California, Bernard Trainor laid out a rustic stairway, *right*, leading from the pool to the cabana and the house using slabs of natural limestone set into a grassy slope.

INSIDE STORY
DANISH MODERN

Midcentury modern Scandinavian landscape was chiefly known for its reverential treatment of the natural environment. Meadows, woodlands and water margins were incorporated and touched only lightly in the creation of parks and gardens. In Denmark, this prevailed to some extent (think of Jens Jensen and the "Prairie School"). But in the midcentury modern period, there emerged a different school of thought led by architects like Troels Erstad, Arne Jacobsen and Carl Theodor Sørensen. Led by their belief in the garden as art they took a humanistic approach, placing people at the center of the landscape and appropriating elements of the bucolic Danish farming landscape to create spaces that echoed the formal order of the Renaissance garden.

Troels Erstad, in his plan for a small private garden, *below,* laid a grid of plant edged pavers surrounded by hedgerows, each of one sort: hawthorn, rose, and so on. Erstad was held in high regard by his fellow modernists but died young, aged 38, never reaching his full potential. His colleague Sørensen, however, was by far the most influential, his life spanning the decades between the Arts and Crafts period to beyond the midcentury modern years. He shares many characteristics with his contemporary Thomas Church: an appreciation of formalism in the creation of livable, comfortable domestic gardens, a philosophy he brought to his many public projects. Yet he had a long-standing engagement with curvilinear forms—circles, ovals, spirals and arcs—which featured in a number of his most important designs.

The simple oval garden *opposite below right* bisected by a gentle zigzag path is a good example. Perhaps his best-known project and one that had wide influence on public landscapes is the Allotments at Naerum, north of Copenhagen, pictured *opposite above.* Built in 1948, the allotments are composed of forty individual garden plots approximately eighty by fifty feet in size arranged to follow the contours of the rolling slope. The site echoes the circular enclosures of Iron Age Saxon villages, and the ancient Austrian grave sites at Hallstatt, a reference, maybe, to Sørensen's knowledge of landscape ethnography and history. The garden tenants were permitted to incorporate their own garden buildings, the intention being to encourage personal expression, although Sørensen did provide guidelines.

Contemporary Danish design draws from this heritage, as seen in the garden *below right* and *opposite below left* designed by Britta Vestergaard at Arcvision. "My goal is to create gardens and parks that activate people, and create places where peace and rest in Nature can be found." Part of a new housing development, planners deliberately left "wedges" of woodland between properties, with the formal garden worked into this informal frame. Schooled in the post-war modernist style, but with attention to international garden history and the continuum of design, she recognizes Sørensen as a key influence: "For me he is the essence of Danish landscape architecture… he was not dictated by the form of the place, but instead he created interior space that has its own simplicity and life that sets it free from the surrounding landscape."

Clutter is a thing of the past, and midcentury modern's simple lines and easy-going practicality suit today's style of living. Knoll's canvas butterfly chairs, *right*, take pride of place next to a Donald Wexler pool; an aluminum table and upholstered chair from the Eames Group lift a small balcony space, *above*; and the simple outline of perennially popular wire frame furniture pieces compliments the pool terrace of an Eliot Noyes-designed house, *opposite*.

MAKE IT MIDCENTURY, BUT MAKE IT YOURS

The invention of the wheel changed the way people lived. It was the first stop on the road to the industrial revolution, but its main impact was to take the grind out of daily tasks—from moving building materials to a new site to delivering food to market. One can only imagine how having a wheel signaled to your neighbors that you were part of the new generation. It might seem a stretch to say that the wheel had similar significance in the midcentury modern period. Mobility equaled modernity, and pieces of furniture wheeled and thus easily movable were all the fashion, particularly for anyone adopting the outdoor lifestyle. A drinks cart on wheels was a must-have item and, like the car in the driveway with its white-wall tires, sent a signal of having arrived at the good life.

Outdoor furnishing and decor has come a long way since the early days of midcentury modern outdoor living. In the period of optimism and experiment following the end of the Second World War, it wasn't just the building trades that benefited from the material developments borne of the war effort. Many factories and producers turned their attentions to interior and, naturally enough, exterior design, and to furnishing the new homes being built. Here was a ready market, and it was a hungry one, with a huge appetite for fresh, new designs that underlined the new sense of confidence and a readiness to have fun.

Today, when we look at midcentury modern period furnishing, there is humor and wit in the design. Relieved of the ornate,

TODAY, WHEN WE LOOK AT MIDCENTURY MODERN PERIOD FURNISHING, THERE IS HUMOR AND WIT IN THE DESIGN

decorated hangovers from the late nineteenth century, it was all about function and form: purposeful and simple. Yet there wasn't a sense of austerity about it. Shapes were sinuous and "organic," drawn from nature, or clean and geometric. Even in the materials used there is playfulness, teased out by designers who rose to the challenge. Best known among these is perhaps the husband and wife design team, Charles and Ray Eames. Those fiberglass bucket-shaped chair seats were inspired, it is said, by the nose-cones of fighter jets, and were made with the same material. (In my family kitchen the chairs, while not Eames originals, were certainly inspired by them—made of fiberglass, luridly turquoise, and circled around a kitchen table, the Formica top of which was supported by legs of bent aluminum tubing—serviceable but cheerful!) Here was furniture that could move indoors or out with ease and without raising eyebrows.

In contrast to the ease with which furniture could be moved in or out, both physically and because the materials from which it was made were weather resistant, were the use of futon-like cushions and stacks of throw-pillows. Scattered on the patio and around the pool, they emphasized the relaxed, "taking-it-easy" vibe.

As described earlier, Garrett Eckbo designed his own garden using Alcoa aluminum to create screens and shades—even Frank Lloyd Wright used aluminum sheeting to surface the walls in his private bathroom at Taliesin West. Diners around the world

It's too soon to say if midcentury design is forever, but indications are in favor of it. Efficiency was a byword, and Ralph Rapson's sketch *opposite* for a selection of wheeled and folding furniture—easily portable and made from upcycled, post-war materials—is more serious than tongue in cheek.

Ray and Charles Eames designed furniture that has been widely admired and mimicked, with good reason. Their dining room chairs *above* are sleek and low-maintenance. Made today from molded polypropylene rather than fiberglass, as was the case for the 1950s originals, they can be wiped clean with a damp sponge.

NAMES TO RECKON WITH

After the Second World War, Robert Brown (of Brown Jordan) and Walter Lamb embarked on a collaboration; Brown was a manufacturer, Lamb an established and respected designer based in Hawaii. Brown determined that he could successfully market a range of patio furniture made from upcycled brass piping and rope cord salvaged from the Navy shipyards at Pearl Harbor. He approached Lamb with his idea, and in 1947 the Walter Lamb "Bronze" collection was launched, so named for the patina the brass tubing developed over time. There could hardly be a piece of furniture that fit so appropriately into its setting and its time; original pieces that come up for auction today are enchanting. There is an innocence to the materials from which the furniture is made; the brass frames

that have weathered into a dusky blue green and rope that has aged and softened. It's basic and serviceable, yet the corners of the table and chair frame are softly curved; the rocker arms curlicue in on themselves and the recliner's graceful s-curved side frame is pure elegance.

Another post-war commission that led to the creation of some easy-care furniture came when Kellett Aircraft Corporation commissioned Ralph Rapson (his drawing on page 82 includes a whimsical little helicopter, perhaps inspired by Kellet's autogiros designs). Minnesota-based, Rapson was closely involved with the Cranbrook Academy of Art and had taught architecture at Yale. For Kellet he designed the Equipment for Living line of patio furniture that went into production in 1945. A Rapson sketch promoting a line of garden furniture includes a wheeled

cart to deliver drinks, snacks and whatever else might be required by the homeowner as they lounged on their sunny patio (see previous page). The tubular frame furniture supporting the seat material is reminiscent of Lamb's work for Brown Jordan; one differing touch is the cowhide used for the deckchair sling. This is perhaps a nod to other designers including Ray and Charles Eames and Mies van der Rohe, who upholstered some of their pieces with animal hide to add a touch of primitive pattern and texture.

Very much in keeping with the twenty-first-century desire to be environmentally minded, and to repurpose materials where possible, Walter Lamb's prototypes for "Bronze" deck furniture from the 1940s began life as navy yard salvage, although in this case its re-use was motivated by economy rather than ecology.

Harry Bertoia's "diamond" wire-frame chairs, *opposite*, which he designed for the firm started by Florence and Hans Knoll, are possibly the most widely recognizable pieces of midcentury modern design. His background as a sculptor and jewelery maker is evident in the form-fitting shape of the chairs and the faceted arrangement of wires.

FOLK ART TABLETOP PIECES JOSTLED FOR ATTENTION ALONGSIDE SLEEKLY DESIGNED SCANDINAVIAN VASES

suddenly found the futuristic appeal of quilted aluminum much to their customers' liking. And spun aluminum made into carafes, tumblers, martini glasses and shakers in bright colors was extremely popular for outdoor tabletops: unbreakable, the exteriors dripped invitingly with condensation.

In the early 1960s, one of the top retailers of midcentury modern household goods was Design Research. The first shop was opened in 1953 in Cambridge, Massachusetts, and the shops quickly spread to other major cities. It became the premier "lifestyle" shop for those at the cutting edge of modernist-influenced domesticity, but one that emphatically did not revere the hard-edge, monochrome Bauhaus diktat. This was form in jellybean

colors, textures that enticed you to reach out and touch; folk art tabletop pieces jostled for attention alongside sleekly designed Scandinavian vases. It was an Aladdin's cave.

I visited the New York shop in the late 1960s, but a few years later was a frequent shopper at Habitat – London's answer to Design Research. I enthusiastically kitted out my first home from its range of Scandinavian-inspired furnishings and tribal rugs. Habitat was established in 1964 by British designer Terence Conran, and along with Heals, mobilized contemporary design and craftsman-made pieces to push mass-produced wartime utility furnishing, post-war G-Plan furniture, flocked wallpaper and Axminster Spotlight carpeting to the curb.

The freedom of midcentury modern design went beyond the home and garden, extending to women's fashion. Playsuits, pedal-pusher pants, T-shirt tops and revealing sundresses—a few of which are shown here—signalled a new freedom for women. Designer Claire McCardell revolutionized the womenswear market by introducing active but feminine sportswear and developing the concept of ready-to-wear. *Time* magazine's 2 May 1955 cover story confirmed her enduring influence on international fashion.

Fashion forward

Claire "Kick" McCardell was an all-American girl and a fashion design graduate of the New York School of Fine and Applied Art (later, Parsons School of Design). A protégé of Townley Frocks, she made her first trip to the Paris fashion shows in 1930, and while everyone else was catching inspiration from the runway, McCardell took her lead from what real people were wearing in the street—a common enough thing to do today, but she was perhaps one of the first designers to do so. It could be said that her clothes were for living: she developed a line of sportswear and interchangeable separates that could adapt easily into any social situation. Her famous "Popover" dress was in fact designed in response to a

magazine challenge to create a dress that could be worn in the kitchen and then to a cocktail party. It had a pocket designed specifically to carry a potholder and it was a big success.

Unlike other designers during the Second World War, McCardell was unaffected by textile shortages, as she had already been designing successfully with the fabrics that were then available, chiefly inexpensive cotton knits and denim. When high heels were in short supply, she put her models in ballet slippers—the start of a collaboration with Capezio ballet shoes, and a craze among young women. (Even I wore Capezios in high school during the mid-1960s!)

McCardell is credited with having introduced the concept of American sportswear; she understood that the new mode of

Bob Dylan's 1964 release "The Times They Are a-Changin'" was an anthem for the midcentury modern period, a change cemented by the 1960 election of John F. Kennedy as president. With his wife, Jackie, the "Camelot" couple embodied the new approach to living. In the 1960 photo *opposite right*, she is wearing the Marimekko sundress that put the textile house on the cultural map. Bright and bold, (even if Jackie's dress appears demure now, it didn't then), the Finnish firm's products injected just the right amount of "pop" and excitement into midcentury designs for living, *above* and *opposite left*.

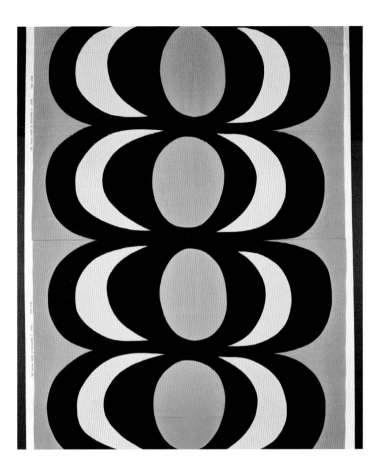

EASY-TO-WEAR YET FASHIONABLE,
CHEERFULLY COLORED OR
INVENTIVELY CUT MIDCENTURY
MODERN CLOTHING WAS THE
TENT POLE AROUND WHICH MUCH
OF THE DECORATIVE DESIGN OF
THE TIME REVOLVED

outdoor living demanded easy-care, easy-to-wear clothes. "I like comfort, I don't like glitter," she said. For her, function led form, and dress pattern houses for home-seamstresses couldn't get enough McCardell designs. The awards flooded in, and in 1954 McCardell collaborated with *Time* magazine on a new publication that became *Sports Illustrated*. In May 1955 *Time* devoted a cover article to Claire McCardell and the "American Look," declaring "From America's lively leisure has evolved a new, home-grown fashion." This look was epitomized by McCardell's modern sportswear, which managed to balance comfort and practicality with casual beauty.

Easy-to-wear yet fashionable, cheerfully colored or inventively cut midcentury modern clothing was the tent pole around which much of the decorative design of the time revolved. And in Europe, much of it came from Scandinavia. Marimekko fabric with large—even gigantic—repeat patterns in boldly colored motifs was like a breath of fresh air, one that eventually blew open the doors to the sharply defined geometry of Pop culture. *Sports Illustrated* demonstrated how fashion-forward it was when in 1960 Jackie Kennedy appeared on a cover wearing a Marimekko-fabric sundress as she tooled around in a motorboat with her husband Jack. With that exposure the company's brand became a household word. Today, Marimekko is experiencing a revival, in part no doubt because of the revival of the midcentury modern style and a growing appreciation of timeless design.

From the artisan-made tree root bench on a Florida deck, *above,* to the delicate bamboo side table from south Asia on an Eliot Noyes-designed deck, *right*, and the white plastic drum table on an English terrace that is all about natural materials, small oddities are grace notes, accenting the modernity of the landscape and architecture.

But let's not forget —timeless design, serviceable indoors or out, comes in many forms. And the flip side to advances in industrial design and manufactured goods for the home—and to Bauhausian minimalist aesthetics—was an understanding that the craftsmanship and the beauty of the handmade, artisan object was unique, and if making a cultural statement was your goal, a live edge table made by George Nakashima from a slab of wood he chose especially for you could hardly be bettered.

Along with Bauhaus architects fleeing Nazi persecution, a wave of artists in every genre swept across the Channel into Britain and across the Atlantic into the United States. Suddenly ceramics, weaving and other traditional handcrafts were being taught in universities for the first time. They caught the eye of interior designers who saw in these handmade shapes and their unusual glazes, vivid colors and textures a welcome respite from the stark, dull-colored and hard-edged angles of modernist rooms. Yet in an age when consumerism and mass-produced goods were dominant, it was almost reactionary to include unique, handcrafted objects.

One of the landmarks in the growing popularity of craft design was the tour made of the United States in 1953 by British potter, Bernard Leach, and the Japanese master potter, Shōji Hamada. The pair had been associated since the 1930s, and helped bridge the creative gap between East and West, leaving as lasting an impact on American ceramics as on British studioware.

DESIGN SCHOOLS
AT THE LEADING EDGE

Modernist teaching and theorizing wasn't confined to Harvard and Yale. Innovation in art education was making headway and there were a number of notable schools that developed interdisciplinary programs, bringing together the arts and science through experimentation and "hands-on" learning. Black Mountain College, founded in 1933, was one of the first, and it soon attracted the attention of leading poets, writers, architects, designers, musicians and artists. At the center was artist Josef Albers and his wife Anni, a weaver. A key figure in the Bauhaus movement, Albers soon recruited Walter Gropius, who was no doubt instrumental in fostering the Bauhaus-like blending of the arts.

The architect and visionary designer Buckminster Fuller developed his geodesic domes, and composer John Cage staged his first "happening" at Black Mountain College. Even Albert Einstein was on the staff (as both a guest lecturer and member of the board), as were a number of the leading visual and performing artists of the midcentury. Located in western North Carolina, Black Mountain College's students and teachers operated as a democratic community, sharing in the manual labor of self-sufficiency, and learning together through experimentation with varying art forms.

The Cranbrook Academy of Art, founded in 1922 on an estate near Detroit, Michigan, claims the title of the cradle of American modernism. Indeed some of the leading architects and designers of the twentieth century were associated with the school: Florence Knoll, Jack Lenor Larsen, Charles and Ray Eames, Harry Bertoia and Eliel Saarinen (the Finnish architect who designed the Academy's main building and landscaping), to name but a few. Self-described as a community of artists, its founder George Gough Booth was a Detroit newspaper owner and philanthropist who admired both the aesthetic of hand-crafted goods, as well as the impulse towards social and economic reform that their creation (through honest labor) appeared to nurture.

In the continuum of Arts and Crafts education, from the English movement led by William Morris through to the German Bauhaus, American centers like Black Mountain College, *below,* **in North Carolina and Cranbrook Academy of Art were responsible for advancing modern artistic, intellectual and political thought.**

Handwoven textiles, tableware, and ceramics were particularly popular in the midcentury period, especially the work of Japanese potter Shōji Hamada. His plates, *above left*, date from the mid-1950s. The English potter, Bernard Leach, *above right* in his studio in Cornwall, introduced Hamada to a western audience, and together the two toured art centers and schools in Europe and the United States.

And of course no account of the evolution of a significant period of interior design would be complete without acknowledging the role of print media in promoting it. *Better Homes & Gardens, House Beautiful, Sunset,* and *Good Housekeeping* were just a few of the interior design-specific magazines strewn across coffee tables the world over, and their editors were active in encouraging architects, interior designers, and manufacturers to originate and innovate. They wanted to help their readers fit comfortably and tastefully into the new material world.

Print media holds much of the same allure today, and for midcentury modernistas there are countless magazines (*Wallpaper*, Dwell*) and websites dedicated to the midcentury modern revival. They are full of feature stories about period homes that have been painstakingly restored to their original state or renovated to fit with contemporary tastes while honoring the original design. From the perspective of the garden, it is true that few midcentury modern homes retain their original plan, let alone the original plants—trees come down, shrubs outgrow their space and tastes change. But within this is the opportunity to make decisions and stylistic choices that reflect present day innovations in structural, planting and decorative design. At the heart of the midcentury modern ethos was a desire to make an original and personal statement, and so while adhering to midcentury modern principles, you can very much make your garden your own.

INSIDE STORY
A FAMILY LANDSCAPE

Midcentury homes and gardens had family at the core of their design; rooms were arranged so that children's activities could be monitored, of course, but also as a means of keeping them engaged with the day-to-day of family life. We could learn a lesson from that earlier, "unplugged" generation. Developing this garden in the Netherlands, Studio Toop's landscape designer Carrie Preston made the most of a small site bordering on a canal, designing a garden that satisfied all generations. The adults have their outdoor room; a simple sheltered patio with a built-in gas grill for al fresco meals, a firepit to ward off the damp on cool evenings, and basic but comfortable seating benches, *opposite below*. Elsewhere it's a child's world, complete with sunken trampoline surrounded by soft flowerbeds, a pair of posts to support a hammock (suitable for grown-ups) and a little cabin on stilts edging up to the banks of the canal. From there the kids can sling a bucket to bring in a haul of water or cast a fishing line, survey the garden, and keep an eye on the grown-ups.

INSIDE STORY
FOUND IN TRANSLATION

"This house was clearly more than just 1950s tract-built," says architect and designer Duane Smith of the property in Palm Springs, California that he calls "Chino Canyon." He believed it had been intentionally designed and oriented to take advantage of the site and mountain views, and, notably, had elements that were distinctly Cliff May in style.

In planning the renovation and remodel—adding an extension, a swimming pool and easy-care landscape—Smith drew on his early experience as a student at the Neue Bauhaus, Dessau in the 1990s. There, in the spirit of the original school, he joined five students in a multi-disciplinary program that brought together fine arts, engineering and architecture students on an environmental design project. The experience in what might be called "total design" gave him an understanding of how design touches everything. "Design is a plan for executing," he says, "good design is a well-executed plan."

The Chino Canyon plan began with a desire to revitalize the property; to bring it up to date and to reinstate the midcentury modern aesthetic for which Palm Springs is so loved, but without resorting to the clichés of white kitchens, tangerine walls and shag carpets.

Like any community, Palm Springs goes through cycles, and today's young creatives are looking for more efficient, less ostentatious homes. Ones that are, as Smith puts it, warmer and more redolent of their personalities and priorities. "Desert Modern" describes the style; it has an edge that at Chino Canyon can be seen in its simple furnishings, earthen colors, and wood and Cor-Ten steel finishes.

Shade is necessary in a garden, and in midcentury gardens, the shadows cast across the varied surfaces of landscaping and plants was integral to the design. Take a look at Garrett Eckbo's 1952 design for the Koolish garden in Bel Air, California, *opposite* and *right,* and how he has framed the metal screening and shading. The way he has deployed the materials and manipulated the shadows they cast clearly references abstract painters such as Mondrian and Kandinsky.

A simple overhang above a deck casts a rich pattern behind one of modernism's leading figures, Marcel Breuer, and his wife as they enjoy the California sun in their garden, *above.*

SHELTERING: SCREEN AND SHADE

The signature picture windows of a midcentury modern home, while glamorous, had their drawbacks. Full sun beating in for most of the day faded fabrics and rad interior temperatures. Living in a fishbowl, too, left a lot to be desired. Privacy at the front and shelter at the back was a consideration when planting and decorating for screening and shade.

In keeping with the midcentury aesthetic of keeping it simple, one might think that the easiest way to provide privacy in a typical residential street would be to erect a tall fence. But that doesn't accord with the other principle of sitting a house comfortably in the landscape; barricades do nothing for blending. Most tract housing then (as now) was constructed on level ground, so sight lines were

also level, and the view consisted of the neighbor's yard across the street. Bearing in mind, however, that the eye is easily distracted, a shapely tree and a few shrubs staggered at varying distances from the front of the house to the property line will soon create a screen. Although not solid like a fence, wall or clipped hedge, this will provide enough of a visual barrier to catch the attention of wandering eyes while providing the homeowner with a view of sorts. Remember the concept of shortened perspective—that which is closest to the house front will appear larger in your view than that which is further away. No need to build a curtain-wall around your castle.

It's a different matter behind the house, as this is where the outdoor living takes place. In the close quarters of most ordinary

Ring the changes on screening: narrow wooden slats on a perimeter fence cast a shadow across pavestones, *left*; a screen of grass, *above*, is a simple solution where a solid barrier would be too heavy; climbing annuals trained up a wire-strung frame, *opposite*, make a temporary screen. As the plants mature, the foliage becomes more dense, and as they wilt in winter it disappears—an engaging solution for an aspect that requires plenty of shade during summer, but which needs whatever sun it can receive during the winter.

housing estates privacy is highly valued but space is usually at a premium, so sheltering groves of trees and thick hedges are not on the menu. But fencing is: fences, they say, make good neighbors. However in some communities the homeowners' associations dictate what sort is permissible, and some even forbid fencing (other than building-code-mandated fencing around swimming pools to keep uninvited guests and their children from drowning).

And all too often the fencing material chosen is the ready-made panels from big-box DIY stores, so that every property seems to have a standard issue stockade erected around its perimeter. Cheap, yes, but hardly cheerful. Boards warp and splinter easily, heavy winds blow them over rather than pass through them, and the stain colors

are altogether unattractive—often a bitter orange that no amount of ivy can disguise. And then there is chain-link fencing: sturdy and gulag-like in appearance, its grizzled metal linkage is hard to ignore. Some drape camouflage netting over it, others weave strips of colored plastic through the weft of wires, but it's probably best left to the mercy of ivy.

Just when you're ready to turn your back on creating an outdoor living space, daunted perhaps by thoughts of what it might cost to do something other than fence panel, the inspiration of midcentury modern comes into its own: pierced block screens of breeze blocks or bricks set in open lattice patterns were a favorite screening device of the period, adding a depth and vigor to the garden

The Celanese House in New Canaan, Connecticut, *top*, was designed by Edward Durrell Stone in 1958, and commissioned by the Celanese fiber company as a show home for their products; hence the hyper-modern roof configuration and tracery screens. In its heyday, there were inverted pyramid planters hanging from each skylight, planted with various trailing tropical foliage plants, like an indoor jungle. *House and Garden* featured the house on a 1959 cover, photographed by Pedro Guerrero, Frank Lloyd Wright's photographer of choice.

Concrete bricks set in alternating courses and at angles make a sculptural screen for a Palm Springs house, *left*, and painted bright red, serve the same purpose in a Steve Martino-designed garden near Phoenix, Arizona *above*.

Among the photographs from Susan Jellicoe's album collection is one of a modernist garden, *opposite*. A pierced screen provides an attractive alternative to a traditional garden fence. This garden was designed by D. Lovejoy for Cheal's and displayed at a Chelsea Flower Show, London.

Upright fencing marks the perimeter of this garden in the Netherlands designed by Carrie Preston. Posts are used to delineate internal spaces, without creating barriers.

Opposite, a privacy screen shields the courtyard garden of a Richard Neutra-designed house in Los Angeles, California from public view, but narrow wood slats set edge-on open the view in the garden itself.

"THE PATTERN OR PLAN OF THE NEW GARDEN LAYOUT MUST EVOLVE ROUND THE POSITION OF THE SUN, IN ORDER THAT FULL USE CAN BE MADE OF IT"

schemes along with that sought-after privacy. And the cost was (and still is) reasonable, when calculated according to the number of years bricks or concrete blocks will last you compared to wooden fence panels.

Other options include translucent polycarbonate sheeting in metal frames, as popular now as it was fifty years ago; corrugated metal sheeting, too (decades ago, corrugated asbestos was suggested for its texture and durability, but of course that is no longer an option!) Where once Eckbo experimented with aluminum products, he might have now joined the designers using Cor-Ten steel panels. Think, too, of Wright's desert concrete, and the ancient method of using poured concrete to create textured walls.

Even older construction materials that have fluency in today's language of garden construction include rammed earth and adobe-type walls. These are especially valued where site-appropriate divisions are desired—what could be more relevant than using native soil and rock to make the hardscape sync with the site? These earthen fences have the advantage that they can be painted or stained to extend the decorative color scheme into the fabric of the garden.

In his 1970 book, *The Room Outside*, John Brookes writes, "The pattern or plan of the new garden layout must evolve round the position of the sun, in order that full use can be made of it." He goes on to remark that the spot in the garden where the best

Opposite, the horizontal-slat-fenced entry to a Florida garden ties the garden to its site, referencing the shade houses used throughout the south to shelter tropical plants that prefer semi-shaded growing conditions.

Cor-Ten steel develops a rusted patina, so is being more widely used for garden elements, from plinth-like fencing, *above,* to planters and even paths. Similarly, translucent tempered glass panels *right* and *overleaf,* telegraph sophisticated modernism in today's gardens, while a poured concrete barrier, *above*, is pure sculpture.

If form follows function, let it not be forgotten that fences are for training plants. Doug Hoerr gave a passage through a lakeside home's landscape a sturdy barrier, *opposite above*; it screens views of Lake Michigan but serves at first glance as a background for a generous display of plants around it and on it. On a smaller scale, *opposite below,* a New York roof terrace designed by Jeffrey Erb is rusticated with a wooden trellis-covered wall that will soon be covered by an evergreen trained up against it.

On the other side of the world, in the hills between Canberra and Melbourne, Australia, the Sawmill House designed by Archier architect studio is sheltered by a sequence of sliding screens, modeled on the traditional rice-paper shoji used as room dividers in traditional Japanese homes.

advantage can be taken of the sun may not be at the spot closest to the house, just outside of the patio doors. This is often overlooked when planning the layout of the garden. In a midcentury modern garden, when the whole of the site behind the house was dedicated to outdoor living, shaded seating areas, sun-bathing spots and play areas were accounted for. And where shade is lacking—perhaps it's a new garden and the trees have only recently been planted, or the space is too limited to allow for the shading desired—useful ideas include pergolas, parasols, and sail-shaped sunshades. Horizontal blinds in the style of Roman shades drawn overhead across a terrace will block the sun's rays, yet not entirely kill the light, and allow for plenty of flexibility.

Brookes continues his discussion with advice about screening noise in the urban garden, suggesting that fountains, tinkling bells and the like can do much to distract; in an urban setting it's impossible to achieve silent repose. I would add to John's considerations that noise sources should be considered when locating the conversation and entertaining areas of a garden plan. This I know from my earliest experience making a garden in South-West London, behind our duplex/semi-detached Edwardian house. There was a serviceable stone terrace directly outside the French doors at the back of the house and the kitchen door also opened onto it. I set about making it our outdoor living space, hanging lanterns, filling the area with scented plants and putting a pergola

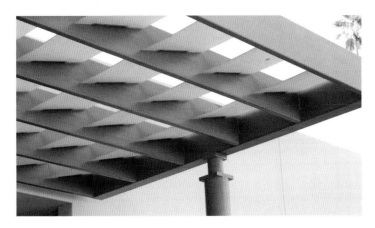

Opposite, a translucent roofing material casts shade but not darkness. Note the corrugated screen at the end of the terrace, too. Robert Royston, who worked extensively with Thomas Church, designed this garden. An open grid, *above*, and a fabric canopy, *right,* are more elaborate than the traditional pergola arrangement of uprights and cross beams, *below* and *below right.*

Screened-in porch areas break up a long glass wall of a San Francisco residence. Note the iconic "nosecone planter" and Knoll Hardoy butterfly chair.

over the area to screen us from the neighbor's back windows. We sat out on the first fine evening after the space was completed and a plane approaching Heathrow came in on its landing course. Nothing much we could do about that other than take a sip of wine as we waited for it to pass. Conversation picked up again only to be halted by the loud and lengthy flush of our neighbor's toilet. Remembering it now, it would have been better to put the terrace at the far end of the garden below a blank wall that overlooked our property, and the garden shed and working parts of the scheme at the back door, beneath the neighbor's bathroom window. Location matters in more ways than one, especially when planning for shelter in the garden.

A square plot does not necessarily a square garden make... Within a frame of curves, British landscape designer Kate Eyre breaks up a London garden into defined spaces for relaxing and entertaining. Planting beds at angles and using a variety of hardscaping materials makes for an attention-grabbing urban landscape.

DEFINING SPACES

"As most of the comforts, and all the elegancies and refinements of life, consist in attention to numerous small matters which are in themselves insignificant, but which, together, compose a beautiful and agreeable whole; so the expression and character of a garden will be cultivated and tasteful, or otherwise, according as its minor features are well arranged and well executed."

By the mid twentieth century, not much had changed in the thinking of garden designers since Edward Kemp wrote these words in his 1850 book *How to Lay Out a Small Garden*. Truthfully, not much has changed as we approach the first quarter of the twenty-first century.

Every garden design begins with a plan, one that is more than "I'm going to make a garden here," but one to which you bring your checklist of needs and your expectations. As in: I need a space to entertain/to relax/to give the children a playspace/ to collect snowdrops... and I expect that I will give all/some/very little of my free time to its upkeep. Doubtless somewhere on the list will be your wish for a garden that makes best use of the site and which complements the house. When I was growing up, I was repeatedly told to do one thing at a time and do it well. Tough on a child possessed of a wide-ranging curiosity, but something that midcentury garden-makers seemed to understand. Tommy Church was one of them: "Do one thing well and let all others be subordinate

On this page, pavers laid widthwise visually expand a long, narrow garden in the Netherlands. By mimicking the shape and rippled surface of the canal beyond, the pavestones extend the garden into the neighboring landscape.

Opposite, a cubist approach to laying out a path and paved area at the water's edge. The individual paving blocks and the way they are arranged emphasize the progression of their size and dimension. This open space and the path leading to it are a counterpoint to the covered terrace from the same garden shown on page 170.

"DO ONE THING WELL AND LET ALL OTHERS BE SUBORDINATE IN SCALE TO THIS IDEA"

in scale to this idea." Which comes down to the notion that if you wish to have a sweeping turf heart to the garden, then don't fuss it up with little flowerbeds and a flotilla of containers. Go big with paved surfaces—bold terraces were preferred over little landing pads where two seated people would be a crowd. Because, he wrote, "The scale of these areas and the simplicity of their unbroken lines are an important consideration in the pleasant relation of the house to the garden."

Russell Page, a Canadian who became one of England's leading midcentury landscape designers advised that, when shaping a garden in the more informal style suited to outdoor living, "a garden which is after all a humanization of nature and intended to be for

'convenience and delight' needs, like all man-made structures, a framework. Its different parts need connecting in some kind of order."

With midcentury modern garden style the order began at the threshold between building and site, where one stepped out of the sliding glass patio doors into the garden. This broad horizontal plane would be the first spatial delineator in the plan, serving, as Page noted, to set the house "firmly in place and suggest stability and repose."

Cliff May houses, as we noted earlier, were built on concrete pads, so the platform was poured as an integral part of the house. In other instances, the terrace was laid as either a patchwork of

Dining al fresco is one of life's primal pleasures. Spaces that are functional yet in tune with their natural surroundings can be as simple as a garden nook in which to enjoy a glass of wine, *right,* or as elegant as a formal table set beneath a grove of trees, as in the Hoerr Schaudt design, *opposite.* In contrast, a modern urban outdoor dining space is cool and refreshing, *above.* White, purple and burgundy flowered perennials edge the seating area with stands of bamboo forming a backdrop to the reflecting pool. The dining table is modeled on the traditional, low, Japanese *horigotatsu,* which allows guests to sit on cushions on the deck, but with their legs extended into the well below the table, rather than tucked under it as is customary. Both gardens designed by Doug Hoerr/ Hoerr Shaudt.

Overleaf, decking connects the living areas and pool of a glass-partitioned Melbourne house designed by Matt Gibson; the tree breaks up the expanse of deck and serves as a visual link with the planting along the boundary wall.

A deck is a platform by another name, although in Swedish landscape architect Per Friberg's hands, a deck lives up to its name, extending the living area into an ocean of wildflowers in a natural heathland around his family home in Ljunghusen, *opposite* and *above*. Friberg designed and built the house in 1960, on a spit of land at the southernmost tip of a Swedish peninsula. Surrounded by water, the temperature rarely reaches frost and the light is pellucid. This no doubt inspired Friberg to design a house that made the best use of its site. He positioned two units, both with broad fenestration, to take full advantage of the site and light from every aspect. The deck connects the two dwellings and has been built around sapling oaks to ensure as little disturbance as possible to the native flora.

In California, Robert Royston positioned elevated decks over a patio, *right,* from where adults could monitor children playing, and in another garden, *below,* extended a platform over the edge of the swimming pool.

Too often, contemporary swimming pools have all the glamour of a public facility: a blue rectangle surrounded by a concrete apron. So much more could be made of them, if only by using the edges as an opportunity for creative expression. The Florentine landscape architect Pietro Porcinai had an inventive approach to landscape solutions, a legacy perhaps of growing up in the land where western garden design and architecture was born. In modern terms, his treatment for the pool edge at Villa Terrazza, where he worked for seven years from 1951-1958, is one of his most engaging. Inspired by abstract painting—especially the work of Wassily Kandinsky—Porcinai bordered the pool with 87 stone circles, some stacked to form diving platforms, others plumbed for jet fountains. Perimeter planting was inspired by Japanese gardens; water lilies, papyri, lotus and other exotic water plants grow in the margin, separated from the recreational pool by the foundation supporting the stone wheels. Ironwork handrails are shaped like trailing vines and tendrils rising up from the water.

irregularly shaped native stone pavers, or—and this is the style most popularly used in reconstructions of midcentury gardens—large square or rectangular concrete pavers, poured on site and then given either an acid wash to smooth the surface, or studded with pebbles to give texture and color. The interstices were filled with ground-hugging edging plants or with gravel; brick, too, was sometimes used as an edging frame. Wooden decks are an option that is perhaps less expensive, but more high maintenance than concrete paving. Redwood, cedar and tropical hardwoods have long been the category leaders, but environmental considerations and production improvements lead many designers to opt for alternatives made from blended wood waste and recycled plastic.

If your garden will include a swimming pool, that will be the next large expanse of hardscape to position, along with a cabana for shade or changing, and if space allows, a paved area around the pool for furniture. A pool, as Tommy Church said, is a place to gather around, to swim in or for "just getting wet if you are hot." Of course, it doesn't have to be a swimming pool that invites the cool reflective surface of water into the texture of the garden; even the smallest of water features can be a destination around which the outdoor living spaces can be organized; a bench by a bubble fountain can be as relaxing as an upholstered recliner at the poolside.

Looking at plans by midcentury designers, it's intriguing to study how pathways through the site were used to define not

Container gardening is taken to a new level in this Australian city garden. Similar in effect to the screen shown on page 159, this is an indoor/outdoor garden that defines the space by casting a flowering curtain across a glass partition, the plants rooted in the shallow, moss-mulched indoor bed; stepping stones through the moss allow for harvesting if climbing beans are used. Ornamental choices include *Lablab purpureus* (hyacinth bean), *Ipomoea purpurea* (morning glory) and hummingbird-friendly *Ipomoea quamoclit* (cypress vine).

But not all space can or should be defined. The antecedents of midcentury modern design respected nature, too, and touched it with only the lightest of hands. One of the earliest garden design precepts was that if the site had a view, there was no need for a garden, or the garden should merely be a frame for what nature provided, *opposite*. That's the ideal, and although we don't all enjoy expansive views, where one exists, embrace it. Don't overwhelm with buildings or with gardens.

Paving can be an excuse to grow more plants, or grow them in unexpected places, which can soften the sometimes unexpressive dullness of gravel and concrete pavers, *left* and *above*. *Right*, in a small urban garden in Denver native stone paving slabs are outlined in self-sown annuals and herbs. *Opposite*, a stretch of gravel— like a carpet runner—breaks up the uniformity of large concrete rectangles, a favorite paving solution in many of today's gardens.

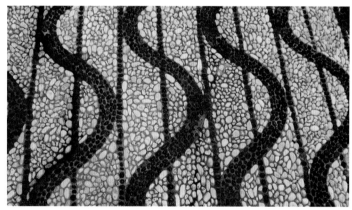

There was a playfulness about midcentury modern landscaping that should not be ignored. And a readiness to experiment that inspired some wonderful garden features, like the abstract pebble mosaics that turn a path or patio into a richly patterned carpet. *Right*, the abstract, paved seating area in a cliff garden at the Vasaparken, Stockholm was designed in 1947 by Erik Glemme, one of the design team working under Holgar Blom, director of the city's Parks Department. Laid in white stone in a foundation of black cobbles, Glemme claimed inspiration for this pattern came from the Moorish gardens such as those at the Alhambra. Similar in period style but simpler in pattern is the pebble mosaic *above*, designed by Pietro Porcinai for a garden in Genova, Italy.

PATHWAYS THROUGH THE SITE
WERE USED TO DEFINE NOT JUST
THE WAY THROUGH THE GARDEN
BUT HOW THE DIFFERENT AREAS
WERE INTEGRATED

just the way through the garden but how the different areas were integrated. Rarely was a path laid in a straight line; paths were connecting arteries between garden spaces, curving gently around islands of planting, leading the eye around corners. In large gardens with expanses of lawn, the path served as a border, wide enough to accommodate two or three people walking abreast. In smaller gardens, where it often doesn't make sense to have a "lawn" and inert or living groundcovers, stepping stones—even cross-sectional slices of cedar—led the way through the layout. A garden might be only fifty feet deep, long, and narrow, but the diagonal lines described by paths and paved areas screened by low hedging or trellis made the space seem larger. Changes in level, too,

contributed to expanding the borders. Short flights of broad steps, either stone or wood beam extend the garden journey; the rise on these steps was shallow, the tread deep enough for just one step at a time, establishing an easy rhythm. At Taliesin West, where levels throughout the house and into the garden frequently change, the rise on most steps was not more than five comfortable inches. Steps are an invitation into the garden, so it's important to make them welcoming, and not just a means to getting up the slope and down again.

INSIDE STORY
HINTING AT DEFINITION

Vertical uprights extending from the framework of a screen porch signal the various areas in a small Dutch garden. Designed by Carrie Preston, the uprights frame the garden view creating little vignettes. In another area not shown here, the uprights support a climbing frame and "tree house" for the children, adjacent to the trampoline, and support a simple plank table for outdoor meals, work or craft projects; parents and children can share the space without getting in each others' way. Tying the whole scheme together are ribbons of perennials set out in the naturalistic manner made so popular by Dutch designers.

Ushering in the modern garden, the English landscape designer John Brookes asked the question, "What do you want to *do* in the garden." Because although plants were, of course, "important" to a garden, what was relevant was its "fitness" for family use. In the midcentury, the three Rs of garden fitness were, Relaxation, Recreation and Reconnection. Little has changed. *Opposite*, a contemporary garden seat nestles in a grove of Mirabelle plum trees screened by a border of *Stipa gigantea*.

Above, a swimming pool is enclosed by a stilt hedge. *Right*, in a garden designed by Bernard Trainor, a richly planted walkway focuses on nature.

A PLAN WITH PLANTS

Trying to write about the plants that characterize a midcentury modern garden is like trying to describe the length of a piece of string. Until after the Second World War, plants had been simply the supporting props on a stage set to dramatize the house and provide an outdoor setting for the people who lived within. Tommy Church captured it perfectly when he titled his seminal landscape design book of the period *Gardens Are for People*.

This may have been more pertinent to gardens in the United States than to those in Europe, and England especially, where it always struck me that we were divided not just by our common language but by the way in Britain gardens were for viewing, while in the USA they were for living. Of course large British properties had dedicated areas for games, but they were set to one side and separated from the "garden"; smaller gardens' vegetable plots were tucked away, and flowerbeds were for emphasized for their beauty, shaping the garden picture. One old garden tenet dating from the early seventeenth century was the direction to "make the entrance to the garden from the best room of the house." And that's as close as it got to an indoor-outdoor lifestyle until well into the twentieth century, when notions of the picturesque were discarded in favor of actually making the garden a part of the space for living.

John Brookes, who began his work in the early 1960s and who today has an international reputation, wrote a thought-provoking

WHAT MIDCENTURY MODERN DESIGNERS WERE PROMOTING WAS A GARDEN... WHERE ONE COULD ESTABLISH "SOME SORT OF CONTACT WITH PLANTS"

guide to gardening aimed at a people rebuilding their lives and homes as they recovered from the Blitz. Visiting London as a child in the late 1950s, there were still, I recall, bombed-out lots where once elegant Georgian row houses stood. Tower blocks were being erected at a rapid pace to house the dispossessed. It was grim. But it was, as Brookes recognized, high time for a fresh way of thinking about how we were to live. He authored a series of books, published by Queen Anne's Press in association with The Gardening Center at Syon Park in South-West London. In one, titled *Living in the Garden*, Brookes set out to describe a new purpose for the garden, and while eschewing the Californian ideal of a sun-baked patio around a glistening blue swimming

pool, recognized that what midcentury modern designers were promoting was a garden for all of life's activities, from the joyful to the mundane. From a place to watch the children wheel around on tricycles, to a spot where the rubbish could be burned, and also where one could establish "some sort of contact with plants." In Brookes's opinion, this was a life-affirming event: "Man seems to need at all stages of his development a presence of *growing* things." He wrote this in the introduction to the next book in the series, *Garden Design and Layout*.

 This slim volume is the how-to manual of its time, as pertinent today as it was then in admonishing his readers to decide what they want. What do you want to *do* in the garden? Which *activities* will

Give the planting character by introducing dramatic contrasts in foliage size, shape and color, as in the design *opposite*.

John Brookes's own gardens at the Clock House, Denmans, in Sussex, England have greatly influenced the evolution of contemporary landscape design, and introduced to designers and gardeners worldwide the concept of informality married to planned and purposeful planting. His book *Room Outside*, first published in 1969, goes further than any other of its time in presenting the whys and hows of creating modern gardens in thorough and accessible terms for home gardeners, not just in Britain, but also in the United States.

Midcentury landscape design and architecture certainly put people in the center of frame, but it would be wrong to think it was done to the exclusion of plants. In fact, the relaxed groundplans and affinity for native and site-appropriate plants extolled in the post-war years continues to inform gardeners now. *Opposite*, in a Californian garden, succulents, cacti and other plants from semi-arid regions are woven together through a matrix of clump-forming grasses.

Architecture and plantsmanship intersected when Flavin Architects worked with Zen Associates to design and build a freestanding conservatory as a bonsai studio. The result bears strong influences of Japanese design filtered through Philip Johnson's famous Glass House.

you entertain? Assess the virtues and shortcomings of the site; get out the pencil and paper and list, sketch and dream. Brookes was targeting the owner of a small garden that was probably part of a new development. Given the never-ending need for housing and expansion on both sides of the Atlantic, what he wrote then, rooted as it was in the new midcentury modern way of life, has relevance to today's homeowner.

Reading Church's *Gardens are for People* along with Brookes's books it is clear that they shared many of the same design principles when it came to planting a garden. Brookes warned against "do-it-yourself design packs [...] mass-produced screen walling [...] plastic carpets—like grass and false flowers." (Did he,

in 1960, see the big box DIY stores coming?) For his part, Church advised, "The garden owner is being constructive about his problems when he analyzes what he really wants as disassociated from what tradition may have convinced him he ought to have [...] There are no set rules, no finger of shame pointed at the gardener who doesn't follow an accepted pattern."

Both were for a sensible use of plants, recommending most strongly that they not be pushed up against boundary lines, or squashed along the foundations of the house. "The relationship between the house and garden is maintained and emphasized by light, air, and visual space flowing freely from one to the other." In other words, Church advocated for a few plants, well chosen and

Trees and shrubs are the bones of a garden layout. *Above,* a rooftop oasis overlooking Central Park, New York borrows from the nearby tree-filled landscape. *Left*, a canopy of evergreen oaks and a carpet of dwarf mundo grass make the landscape for a contemporary San Antonio, Texas, house.

Opposite: Although large-scale plants may grow to obscure an well-designed entranceway, they can also act as street-front privacy screens.

purposefully disposed. "Too much enthusiasm in planting at the base of a house can do a garden in quicker than anything else." I'd say this is generally true about many things, but in this instance he was warning against obscuring the lines of a well-designed house. Gertrude Jekyll, the doyenne of romantic Edwardian gardens, did the same, when she advised against letting ivy overrun the brickwork and carved stone ornament of old houses, thus hiding their structural beauty.

Structural planting, wrote Brookes, was integral to the success of a garden plan and was applied only after the design was settled. It began with trees and shrubs, a few of which could be selected as eye-catching specimens, but the rest

of which "will probably be *bold* and *simple* [author's italics], for you are creating the bones of your layout." Trees and evergreens were of paramount importance, used as screening and shelter, or as statements. Their form or outline, bark and foliage would underpin the garden. If the site had the good fortune to contain healthy mature trees, they should be respected and the house built around them in deference to their position, so that they could later be incorporated into the garden plan. Shrubs formed the understory and were best thought of as screening, but again should be chosen for their beauty of shape and foliage, if not their suitability to be grown as a hedge. Perennials, grasses, groundcovers also all had their function in Brooke's plan, either

Images of gardens from Paul J. Peart's book 1963 book *Pictorial Plant Guide for Mild Region Landscaping* illustrate the importance of "cornerstone" plants. Interestingly, the book gives no horticultural or design recommendations, just plant names and visual inspiration. *Above*, California fan palm, *Washingtonia filifera*, makes a spreading mound in the corner, a contrast to the sinewy verticals of ocotillo, *Fouquieria splendens,* a Sonoran Desert native. *Left*, individually planted clumps of umbrella papyrus, *Cyperus alternifolius* stand in for the more typical bamboo, and are easier to manage. *Below*, the vast shield-shaped leaves of the king philodendron, *Philodendron eichleri,* obscures the front entrance.

Opposite, in Karl Foerster's garden, the sharp color and mounded form of *Hakonechloa macra* 'Aureola' marks the rise of steps on a path.

massed or as anchor plants. But it was the "plan" that they served, rather than the other way around.

Plants naturally

Some years ago, in my book *The Autumn Garden*, I quoted Jens Jensen, who wrote that the building blocks of the garden were "the contours of the earth, the vegetation that covers it, the changing season, the rays of the setting sun, and the afterglow, and the light of the moon." Jensen, as described on pages 23–27, took his inspiration for the projects he developed directly from the site, so much so that his hand is hardly discernible in the landscape. A number of landscape professionals working with architects during the midcentury held to this ideal. This approach is most adaptable to larger pieces of land, or so you might think. But in the late 1970s a new "natural" approach to garden design was evolving out of the pre-war work done in Germany by Lange, Foerster, and later, Richard Hansen at Weihenstephan. It was promoted to the world at large by international garden festivals, still hosted today, by a different German town each year. These festivals provide the opportunity for growers, designers, artists and craftspeople to display their talents; for growers it is an opportunity to introduce their newest plant cultivars. And when the festival ends, the park remains a public asset!

Describing her work for the 1983 festival at Munich's Westpark, landscape architect Rosemarie Weisse explained that

PERENNIAL SCHEMES WERE DISPOSED IN DRIFTS, THEIR EDGES BLURRING AND MERGING INTO EACH OTHER SO THAT GROUPS OVERLAP, FLOWERING AND FADING IN WAVES

The naturalistic style of planting that brings together compatible perennials with ornamental grasses was developed in pre-war Germany but brought to the attention of contemporary garden designers by the work of Rosemarie Weisse in the public gardens at Munich's Westpark, *previous page.* Richard Hansen did the early work developing the style in his trial gardens at the Weihenstephan, now a teaching and research garden of the Fachhochschule, Friesing, near Munich, *above left*.

In 1992, Ingolstadt was the site of the Bavarian state garden show—the Landesgartenshau. Areas of the park (photographed *above right and opposite above* in 1994) were designed and planted according to the principles of the New Perennial style. In 2020, Ingolstadt will host the festival once again. An artist's impression for the new water terrace area *opposite below* proposes a cleaner, more structured look, much in line with other aspects of midcentury modern design.

her initial brief for the garden was to display the diversity of day lilies, an adaptable native of the American prairie. "It was decided to use them with different habitats and in combination with a wide range of plants." Used variously as a woodland edge species, naturalized in a meadow, or in steppe or open border, she wrote that the ultimate aim was to show "how to naturalize plants, based on their natural habitats" whilst not losing sight of aesthetic.

In contrast to what has been the standard technique for planting perennials—setting them in large clumps—Westpark's perennial schemes were disposed in drifts, their edges blurring and merging into each other so that groups overlap, flowering and fading in waves, "just like one would find it in nature." This was a new way of

designing with plants, combining sustainability with creativity. It was a technique for achieving a low-maintenance, natural looking garden by exploiting the sociability of plants, growing them in mutually compatible, self-sustaining communities. It is also one that can be geared to a single flowerbed or an entire garden.

Weisse grouped the plants by habit: tuft-forming (the tall grasses that dominate a grouping); medium-height perennials used in groups as they would appear in nature (daylilies, sedums, asters, hostas etc.); and ground-covering plants. Spacings were generous for the Westpark garden; 1–2 plants per square meter for large specimens, 5–6 for medium height, and 7–10 for groundcovers, the latter two forming a matrix through which the larger perennials

Beth Chatto has long been one of England's guiding lights in the union of plantsmanship and design, as is expressed in her garden near Chelmsford, Essex—one of the driest, sunniest parts of the country, bedeviled by persistent, desiccating winds in both spring and summer. Beginning in 1960, she and her husband have since transformed the four or so acres of neglected farmland they started with into gardens that are built on the influential premise of "know your site and plant accordingly."

In her 1993 plant catalogue, Beth states her "basic principles of gardening," beginning with: "To provide plants as far as possible with the kind of conditions for which nature has fitted them." In her hands, a spring-fed ditch was enlarged to form a bog garden for water-loving marginals, *opposite*, and a car park was transformed into a sunbaked gravel garden, *above* and *overleaf*. Growing a selection of perennials that demanded arid conditions was a revelation to a new generation of gardeners facing climate change.

grow. They were mulched with gravel and fed at long intervals from first planting in 1983. In 1994, when I attended the symposium from which these notes come, the garden was holding up well.

Titled "New Trends in Planting Design," the symposium was the first in a series organized by Schoenaich Rees Landscape Architects, and was held at the Royal Botanic Gardens, Kew. Other speakers at this conference included Klaus Wittke, who described the history of naturalistic planting in Germany with specific reference to the Weihenstephan trial gardens; James Hitchmough, who since that time has steered British amenity planting in a naturalistic direction with seed-sown meadow carpets of selected annuals; and Beth Chatto.

Now an internationally revered plantswoman, Chatto's education as a gardener began in the 1960s at her property in a windswept corner of Essex in the east of England. Chatto's husband, Andrew, had conducted a "life-long study of the natural homes of many of our garden plants, trees and shrubs," she wrote, and she set about making naturalistic gardens by trial and error, working always to the principle that the best approach is to suit the plants to the site and to each other.

By the mid-1990s, there were four main garden areas: a dry shade garden beneath trees and shrubs, an open sunny border garden located in moist meadow soil, a water garden of "marginal planting around four ponds made by damming a spring-fed ditch"

(turning lemons into lemonade!), and a dry, Mediterranean-style garden particularly well-suited to the conditions in East Anglia—the sunniest, least rainy region in England, as I can testify having gardened there for fifteen years.

Not surprising then that the Beth Chatto Gardens were my source of planting inspiration. And that had been the case long before I moved from London to Norfolk. The Chatto stand at the Chelsea Flower Shows during this period provided the inspiration for the planting schemes that I aspired to. Between 1977, the year I started gardening, and 1986, when we moved to Norfolk, I learned from each stand the meaning of habitat gardening. Chatto discontinued her appearances at the Chelsea Flower show some

years ago, but at plant fairs in her own garden I have seen that the "island gardens" are once again being created to admire and inspire.

"The New Trends" symposia described on page 207 were intended not just to introduce what was being done elsewhere in the world, but to help British gardeners find a modern language of garden design and planting. New gardeners were seeking new forms through which to express their creativity, and that went beyond the confines of Edwardian-style formalism inspired by the cult of Gertrude Jekyll and Edwin Lutyens, or the romantic historicism of Tudorbethan gardens.

Forward momentum had stopped and something fresh was needed. Midcentury modernism in interior and exterior design

Contemporary gardens in Southern California and the desert Southwest have an air of being "nongarden." A jokey description of landscapes planted almost entirely with cacti and rocks, palms and palo verde trees—a plant palette that needs little "gardening" to exist. The Neutra/Kaufmann garden, *opposite*, has hardly changed in fifty years, and boulders and Sonoran Desert scrub nearly disguise the classic Palm Springs modern home overlooking the Coachella Valley, *above*.

Those sparse elements, though, can form the basis of some inventive planting details. *Above*, clumping grasses in a bed of river mulch form a natural shag carpet, while dramatic aloe plants drift in a sea of golden barrel cacti making for an eye-catching front garden, *below*. And then there's the irony of planting not only a hedge of saguaro cacti, but setting out a specimen in the middle of a water feature, as Steve Martino did in the Palm Springs garden pictured *left*.

INSIDE STORY CONNECTING THROUGH TIME AND SPACE

Peter Zumthor, the award-winning Swiss architect, claims that he was trained in the school of modernism, with its emphasis on the supremacy of space in design. For the 2011 Serpentine Gallery Pavilion in London, Zumthor modeled a space rooted not in midcentury architecture, but in one of the oldest building and landscape forms: the enclosed garden, or cloister garden, of the early medieval Christian world.

Piet Oudolf, one of the leading "New Perennialist" designers, was called in to design the garden; given Oudolf's usual format of wide open spaces and projects that mature over years, planting a garden that would exist for only three months in a restricted space was a challenge. But the result was an installation of complex, ephemeral beauty.

From the outside, the pavilion was a simple black box, but inside was a roofless core centered on a flower-filled garden. Walking into the bright, sunlit space encouraged quiet contemplation with a focus on the transient beauty of nature.

Cloisters and their gardens are one of the earliest forms of landscape design in the western world. The inner sanctum of the monasteries were first a meditative space and later a refuge, not just for the monks, but also for plant knowledge of the ancient world, as civilization appeared to recede into darkness. In tribute to this history, Oudolf's plant list for the pocket garden describes a number of plants that are modern ornamental cultivars along with ancient medicinal herbs like *Sanguisorba* (burnet), *Astrantia* (masterwort), *Aconitum* (Wolf's bane), and yellow-flowered wild parsnip.

Dutch artist Ton der Linden was one of the pillars of the Dutch Wave, and his borders, *above* (photographed in 1995), were the most painterly and most color-driven of the style. In planting, he mingled plant heights, looked for strong vertical stems, and placed tall growers to the front as "see-through" plants.

As plants fade, *right*, the dried stems create a gossamer curtain, blending together flower heads chosen for their varying sizes and shapes, and of course colors. Perennials, bulbs and grasses are planted not in clumps or drifts, but mingled so that as they fill and mature, light is captured and brought into the garden picture.

filled the bill. The *lived-in* garden, with its limited plant palette and focus on hardscaping and structure, presented new homeowners with the landscape they could manage.

The "New Perennialists" gave plant lovers a path into the future that satisfied their needs to be relevant and sensitive to the environment, and redefined what made a garden beautiful. This was a language of design that made an easy crossover into the United States, where naturalistic gardens of the sort promoted by Jens Jensen and modernist architects were already at home. Finally, there seemed to be a mutual respect between British and American gardeners, where there had previously been disdain on the one hand and a cultural cringe on the other.

As we come to realize that our ability to expand outstrips our ability to sustain, where do we turn next in the quest for a modern language of landscape architecture and design? In 1976, at the tail end of the midcentury modern period, Houston-based architect Roger Rasbach proposed a new model for living in his designs for the Provident Home. Using Structural Insulated panels, solar energy, rainwater storage systems, recycling processes and purpose-built communities where family homes were grouped in small villages, Roger painted a picture for a lifestyle that made benign, positive use of scientific advances, that had an undisguised respect for the natural resources and beauty of our world, and encouraged people to live within their

Occasionally all it takes to define a garden is a chair and a few plants, and that is exactly what struck me when I came across this quiet moment in the late Henk Gerritsen's riotous Priona Garden in the mid 1990s. The Dutch Wave was only a ripple gathering momentum at that point; the New Perennial garden symposiums were yet to come. And Henk, as I learned, was at the forefront of this new, much-needed style of shaping a garden; a garden without borders, one that is full of contradictions and unexpected approaches to design. At Priona, the result was a sensory overload of abstract topiary forms that hedged flowering meadows, where select perennials were put in their place by "weeds," and where art and nature held hands. But this little moment—a watering can, a container packed with all sorts of cacti awaiting attention and an unpretentious striped canvas deck chair—sums up the contentment of gardening to be found in realizing one's most personal expression. That is the essence of the modern garden.

THE MIDCENTURY MODERN JOY FOR LIVING, ENTHUSIASM FOR THE FUTURE, AND SOCIAL AWARENESS IN COMMUNITY AND FAMILY LIFE ARE STILL RELEVANT

means and the means of the planet. Writing in his 1976 treatise, *The Provident Planner: A Blueprint for Homes, Communities, and Lifestyles*, he said, "Willy-nilly, whether we like it or not, frugality and provident planning will be forced upon us, if we don't volunteer. The post-1976 architecture will resemble a revival of our rural, regional beginnings… simple unadorned shapes… houses oriented to take advantage of the natural assets of the building site. These are on the way, we have no choice."

In his last years, Roger and I talked about collaborating on a book, *The Provident Garden*, that would elaborate on his plans for building small, efficient homes within gardens designed for pleasure, and for open community spaces that would provide the all-essential connection to the land. Were he alive today, I think he would be as tremendously excited as I have been to witness not just that much of what he advocated for is on the agenda today, but also that the midcentury modern joy for living, enthusiasm for the future, and social awareness in community and family life are still relevant.

"Modern," wrote Thomas Church, "can be revived as an honest word when we realize that modernism is not a goal but a broad highway." I hope this book, and the work of the landscaper architects and garden designers it contains demonstrate that we are on the way, honoring the legacy of the post-war past but shaping a blueprint for a more inclusive, sustainable future.

Adamson, Paul. *Eichler: Modernism Rebuilds the American Dream.* Gibbs Smith, Salt Lake City, 2002.

Birnbaum, Charles. *Preserving Modern Landscape Architecture II: Making Postwar Landscapes Visible.* Spacemaker Press, Washington, DC, 2004.

Brookes, John. *Room Outside: A New Approach to Garden Design.* Penguin Books, London. 1969. (revised ed. Thames and Hudson, USA. 1985)

Brookes, John. *A Place in the Country.* Thames and Hudson, London. 1984.

Church, Thomas. *Gardens are for People.* Reinhold Publishing, New York. 1955 (2nd ed. McGraw-Hill, 1983).

Clarke, Ethne. *Infinity of Graces: Cecil Pinsent, an English Architect in the Italian Landscape.* W.W. Norton, London and New York. 2013.

Crowe, Sylvia. *Garden Design.* Hearthside Press, New York, 1959 (USA ed.)

Eckbo, Garrett. *Home Landscape: The Art of Home Landscaping.* McGraw-Hill, New York. 1978 (revised and enlarged ed.)

Eckbo, Garrett. *Landscape for Living.* Architectural Record/Duell, Sloan & Pearce, New York, 1950.

Eckbo, Garrett. *Urban Landscape Design.* McGraw-Hill, New York, 1964.

Faragher, John Mack. "Bungalow and Ranch House: The Architectural Backwash of California." *The Western Historical Quarterly* 32:2 (2001) 149-73.

Gibson, Trish. *Brenda Colvin: A Career in Landscape.* Frances Lincoln, London. 2011.

Hansen, Richard and Friedrich Stahl. *Perennials and Their Garden Habitats.* Cambridge University Press, Cambridge. 1993 (4th ed.)

Hines, Thomas S. *Irving Gill and the Architecture of Reform: A Study in Modernist Architectural Culture.* Monacelli Press, New York. 2000.

Imbert, Dorothée. *Between Garden and city: Jean Canneel Claes and landscape modernism.* University of Pittsburgh Press, Pittsburgh. 2009.

Jellicoe, Geoffrey and Susan. *The Landscape of Man: Shaping the Environment from Prehistory to the Present Day.* Thames and Hudson, London. 1987 (revised ed.)

Jellicoe, Geoffrey and Susan. *Modern Private Gardens.* Abelard – Schuman, London. 1968.

Kendle, Tony and Stephen Forbes. *Urban Nature Conservation: Landscape Management in the Urban Countryside.* Thomson Professional, London. 1997.

Lamprecht, Barbara. *Neutra.* Taschen, Köln. 2004

Laskey, Marlene L. *The California Ranch House: Cliff May.* Oral History Program, University of California, Los Angeles. 1984.

May, Cliff. *Western Ranch Houses.* Hennessey + Ingalls, Santa Monica. 1997 (reprint ed.)

McLeod, Mary. "Architecture or Revolution: Taylorism, Technocracy, and Social Change." *Art Journal* 43:2 (1983) 132-47.

Muthesius, Hermann. *The English House.* Crosby, Lockwood, Staples, London. 1979.

Page, Russell. *The Education of a Gardener.* Collins, London. 1962.

Peets, Elbert. *Papers 1883-1983, 1904-1974. Collection 2772.* Division of Rare and Manuscript Collections, Cornell University Library, Ithaca.

Peets, Elbert. "The Landscape Priesthood." *The American Mercury* 01:27 (1927) *94-100.*

Powers, Alan with Alan Crawford and Ronald Leask. *John Campbell: Rediscovery of an Arts & Crafts Architect.* The Prince of Wales Institute of Architecture, London. 1997.

Russell, Virginia L. "You Dear Old Prima Donna: The Letters of Frank Lloyd Wright and Jens Jensen." *Landscape Journal* 20:2 (2001) 141-55.

Schnay, Jerry. *Park Forest: Dreams and Challenges.* Arcadia, Chicago. 2002.

Schoenaich Rees Landscape Architects, ed. "New Trends in Planting Design," *Designing with Perennials Symposium.* Royal Botanic Gardens, Kew. 1994.

Schoenaich Rees Landscape Architects, ed. "New Trends in Planting Design II," *The Perennial Symposium.* Royal Botanic Gardens Kew. 1997.

Soule, George and Vincent Carosso. *American Economic History.* Dryden Press, New York. 1957.

Tishler, William H., ed. *Midwestern Landscape Architecture.* University of Illinois Press, Urbana and Chicago. 2000.

Treib, Marc, ed. *The Architecture of Landscape, 1940-1960.* University of Pennsylvania Press, Philadelphia. 2002.

Treib, Marc, ed. "Thomas Church, Garrett Eckbo, and the Postwar California Garden." *Preserving the Recent Past 2,* ed. Slaton and Foulks. Historic Preservation Education Foundation, National Park Service and Association for Preservation Technology International. 2000.

Treib, Marc and Imbert, Dorothée, ed. *Garrett Eckbo: Modern Landscape for Living.* University of California Press, Berkeley. 1997.

Tunnard, Christopher. *Gardens in the Modern Landscape.* Scribner. New York. 1948.

Wolfe, Tom. *From Bauhaus to Our House.* Farrar, Strauss and Giroux. New York. 1981.

INDEX

Page numbers in *italics* indicate an entry in a caption to an illustration; page numbers in **bold** indicate an entry in a box.

A

Aalto, Alvar **46**, *68*
Abstract House **97**
Aconitum (wolf's bane) **212**
adobe-type design 164
Albers, Anni **150**
Albers, Josef 100–2, *102*, **150**
Alcoa 74
aloes *211*
aluminum 138–43
Anigozanthos (kangaroo paw) **92**
Archier Architect Studio *169*
Arcvision **134–5**
art pieces 113
artistic statements 122–7
Arts and Crafts Movement 17, *29*, 29, 33, 58, 106, **150**
Asian influences *119*, *122*, *128*
Astrantia (masterwort) **212**
atrium *83*
Australian design *186*
  see also Melbourne, Australia
Austrian Union of Settlers and Small Gardeners 104

B

Bailey, Liberty Hyde 18
bamboo *179*
Baron Haussmann 12
Barragán, Luis **114–15**
Bauhaus 33–7, 104, 148, **150**
Bavarian State Garden Show *204*
Bayliss, Roger 68
beachside house *68*
Beaux Arts 29, 37, 73
Belgian Association of Garden Architects 43
Belluschi, Pietro 65
Bennett, Richard 12
Berenson, Bernard 29
Bertoia, Harry *142*, **150**
Bertoia wire chair *91*, 91, *142*
Better Homes and Gardens 151
Birchen's Spring *30*, 30

Black Mountain School 102, **150**
Blom, Holgar *188*
Blomfield, Reginald 17
Bodorff, Ulla 43
Bolles residence *73*
Booth, George Gough **150**
Braun, Ernst *99*
Breuer, Marcel *157*
Breuer, Philip Johnson 37, **38**
Brick Weave House *122*
Broadacre City 27, *27*
bromeliads *132*
Bronze collection **140**
Brookes, John *86*, 164, *169*, *193*, *193*–7, *195*, 198
Brown, Robert **140**
bulbs *213*
Burle Marx, Roberto **117**
burnet *see Sanguisorba*
Buscot Old Parsonage *43*
Butterfly House *111*

C

cacti *197*, *211*
Cage, John **150**
Calamagrostis x *ocutiflora* 'Karl Foerster' *35*
California *197*
California fan palm *see Washingtonia filifera*
Campbell, John Archibald 29, *30*
Canneel-Claes, Jean 43–5, *48*
Capability Brown 51
Capezio ballet shoes 144
Carmel, California *135*
Case Study houses *62*, *62*, *83*
Caudra San Cristóba *114*
Celanese House, New Canaan *158*
Central Park, New York 17, *198*
'Century of Progress' **14**
ceramics 148, *151*
Chatto, Beth **92**, *207*, 207–10
Cheal's *158*
Chelsea Flower Show *158*
Chino Canyon **155**
Chicago *122*
Chicago World Fair **14**
children, gardens for **152**

Church, Thomas Dolliver *57*, *66*, 66, *68*, *68*, *73*, *74*, *99*, 119–22, *128*, **134–5**, *171*, 175, 184, *193*, 197–8
Clearing, The 27
Clément, Gilles *108*
climbers *186*
Clock House, Denmans *195*
cloister garden **212**
clothes fashion 144–7
Coconut Grove, Florida **117**
Cocteau, Jean *101*
Color-Aid paper 102–3
color in design 100–8, *108*, **114–17**, *121*, *127*, *132*, 143, *158*, *214*
Colvin, Brenda 43, 52, *53*, 99
concrete 9, 34, **38**, *53*, *101*, *104*, 111, *117*, 122, 127, *128*, *158*, 163, 164
Concrete House, Melbourne *135*
Congress of Garden Architects 43
Conran, Terence 143
containers *186*
Cooper, Gary *58*
Cor-Ten steel **155**, 164, *165*
Cottesbrooke Manor, Northampton *53*
council rings 23, *24*, 110
courtyards *81*, **97**
Cranbrook Academy of Art **140**, **150**
Crowe, Sylvia 52–3, *53*
cubist design *29*, *84*, *108*, **114**, *176*
Cyperus alternifolius (umbrella papyrus) *200*
cypress vine *see Ipomoea quamoclit*

D

Dalí, Salvador *101*
Danish landscape design **134–5**
day lilies 204
Day, Lucienne *146*
decking *179*, *183*, 184
Degenerate Exhibition, The 36
Denmans, Sussex *86*
desert designs 163, *211*
Desert Modern **155**
Design Research 143
Donnelly residence, California *66*, 68
Drummer's Yard *see* Birchen's Spring
dry garden 210

  see also desert designs
dry shade garden 207–10
Duchène, Achille 43
Dutch Wave, *213*, *215*

E

Eames, Charles and Ray **62**, *91*, *91*, *137*, 138, *139*, **140**, **150**
Eckbo, Garrett *58*, 68–73, *70*, *73*, 74, *74*, 107, 108, *108*, 113, 138–43, *157*, 163
Edwards, Dunn *102*, 103
Eichler color palette *102*
Eichler houses *9*, *81*, 103
Eichler, Joseph *58*, 65, *84*
Einstein, Albert **150**
L'Enfant, Pierre 12
English gardens 35–6
  landscape style 17–18, *37*
Entenza, John **62**
Equipment for Living **140**
Erb, Jeffrey *169*
Ericson, Estrid *104*, 106, 107
Erstad, Troels **134–5**
Eyre, Kate *175*

F

fabrics *see* furnishings; textiles
Fachhochschule *204*
Fair Lane, Michigan 27
Fallingwater, Pennsylvania 23
fan palm *132*
fashion in clothing 144–7
fences *119*, *158*, *162*, *169*
ferns 35, *132*
Festival of Britain 1951 *86*
Flavin Architects *197*
Florida houses **116–17**, 164
Foerster, Karl *35*, 35–6, 50, *200*, 201
Foerster's feather reed grass *see Calamagrostis* x *ocutiflora* 'Karl Foerster'
foliage plants *108*, *195*
Ford, Henry 27
Forest Preserve system 23
Fouquieria splendens (ocotillo) *200*
Frank, Josef 104–7
Freed, Elaine 15
Friberg, Per **46**, *183*

INDEX

PHOTO CREDITS

Front cover image
© Tim Street-Porter/OTTO Archive

Back cover image
© Daniel Hennessy Photo

akg-images:
© DACS/Josef Albers 102

Alamy Stock Photo: Agencja Fotograficzna Caro 32; Arcaid Images 137 right, 149; Arcaid Images © FLC/DACS, 2016 Courtesy of Fondation Le Corbusier 34; Christine Webb 31 below; Lordprice Collection 14; Mira 19; Peter Anderson 68; RWI FINE ART PHOTOGRAPHY 25 below; Stephen Parker 54 left; VIEW Pictures Ltd 138, 212

© Andrew Ashton Photography 101, 130 below

Arcaid Images: Richard Powers 85

Archier Architects 169

Architectural Press Archive/ RIBA Collections 45

© arcvision landscape, Denmark, courtesy of Britta Vestergaard 134 below left, 135 below left

Armando Salas Portugal © Barragán Foundation/DACS 2017, courtesy of the Luis Barragán Foundation 115

Bridgeman Images: Brian Seed 151 right; Private Collection 30 left

Carrie Preston 152, 153, 158 right, 162, 176, 188 above right, 190, 191

Charles Gérard © FLC/DACS, 2016 Courtesy of Fondation Le Corbusier 33

© Chicago Park District 24 above

© Chicago Parks Foundation 25 above

Courtesy of The Clearing Archive 24 below

© Colvin & Moggridge 42, 53

© Country Life Magazine 30 right

© Daniel Hennessy Photo 78

© Darren Bradley/Flickr 119 left

Graphic © Därr Landschaftsarchitekten 205 below

© Denmark Media Center 135 above

© Derek Fell 17, 20–21

© Duane Smith 154, 155

Elbert Peets papers, #2772. Division of Rare and Manuscript Collections, Cornell University Library USA 12, 13

© Ernest Braun, courtesy of Jonathan Braun 6, 98, 109, 170, 177

© Estate of Eliot Noyes, courtesy of Gordon Bruce 38, 39 above

© Ethne Clarke 108, 111 left, 121 above, 128 right, 130 above right, 133 below right, 160 below left, 165 below left, 171 above right, 188 middle right, 193 right, 198 left, 204, 205, 207, 208–209, 211 above left, 213, 215

The Frank Lloyd Wright Foundation Archives (The Museum of Modern Art | Avery Architectural & Fine Arts Library, Columbia University, New York): George Berdan House (4501.001) 18; Living City (5825.007) 26 above; Living City (5825.006) 26 below

GAP Photos: Brent Wilson 81 left, 132; Charles Hawes 202–203; Christa Brand 50, 51; Clive Nichols 91 right; Elke Borkowski 179 below, 192; Howard Rice 206 above; Jacqui Hurst 86 below left; Jerry Harpur 55, 86 above right, 87; Nicola Browne 187; Nicola Stocken 99 right, 179 above; Richard Bloom 196; Suzie Gibbons 35; Tomek Ciesielski 201

Garden World Images: Andrea Jones 195

Getty Images: Andre Kertesz 136; Carol M. Highsmith/Buyenlarge 40–41; Danita Delimont 91 left; David McCabe 144 left; Don Bartletti 110; Frances McLaughlin-Gill 145; Fred Lyon 64; Gabriel Benzur 150 left; Genevieve Naylor 144 left, 150 right; George Silk/The LIFE Picture Collection 39 below; Gerard SIOEN 100; Gordon Parks 57, 61; John Dominis 88, 148 right; Kirk McKoy 126 above; Livia Comandini 116 above; Sports Illustrated 147 right; Thomas D. McAvoy 117 above; ullstein bild 54 right

© Giovani Lunardi Photography 164

Courtesy of Hoerr Schaudt Landscape Architects: Charlie Mayer Photography 118; Henry Joy IV Photography 107 left; Jack Coyier Photography 178; Scott Shigley Photography 168 above

The Interior Archive: Adam Butler 107 right; Fritz von der Schulenburg 113 right; Mark Luscombe-Whyte 59, 142 right; Michel Arnaud 142 below; Simon Upton 163

© Jason Ingram 52

© Jason Liske for Bernard Trainor + Associates 92, 93, 94-95

Jeffrey Erb for Jeffrey Erb Landscape Design 168 below, 171 below right, 198 right

© Jim Bartsch Photographer 80

© Jonathan Buckley 194

Julius Shulman Photography Archive © J. Paul Getty Trust. Getty Research Institute, Los Angeles (2004.R.10) 62, 63, 70, 72, 74, 75, 83, 89 above left, 89 below, 90, 112, 113 left, 119 right, 120 below, 122 left, 128 left, 141, 144 right, 156, 157 right, 171 left, 172, 173, 210

© Karl Dietrich-Bühler 46, 47, 182, 183 above left

© Kate Eyre Garden Design 158 left, 174, 175, 188 above left

Library of Congress, USA © Walter Gropius 36, 37

© Marion Brenner Photography 111 right, 124 above, 159, 189

Courtesy of Matt Gibson Architecture + Design: 180–181; Derek Swawell 126 below right, 133 above; Shannon McGrath 96, 97, 127, 133 below left, 186

© Maynard L. Parker, photographer. Courtesy of The Huntington Library, San Marino, California USA 60, 66

OTTO Archive: Mariko Reed 84, 89 above right, 121 left

© Paola Porcinai 184, 185, 188 below left

© Paul J. Peart 71, 199 above, 200, 211 above right

© Pedro E. Guerrero Archives 2017 22, 124 below left, 157 left, 160 above

© Peter Shepheard 48 above, 122 right, 188 below right, 134 left, 134 above right

© Peter Vanderwarker for Flavin Architects LLC 197

© Roger Foley for Raymond Jungles 116 below, 117 below

San Diego History Center 28

Scala: Christie's Images, London 147 left; DeAgostini Picture Library 151 left

© Scott Hargis Photo 2013, courtesy of Building Lab 129

© Stephen Dunn for Raymond Jungles 131 below

© Steve Hall, Hedrich Blessing 123

© Steve Martino 99 left, 114, 124 below right, 131 above, 160 below right, 165 above, 165 below right, 166–167, 171 above left, 211 below left

© Steven Brooke for Raymond Jungles 81 right, 120 above, 126 below left, 130 above left, 148 left, 199 below

© Steven Wooster 86 above left, 206 below

Courtesy of Surface Design 125

Susan Jellicoe Collection, Museum of English Rural Life, University of Reading UK 161

© Svenskt Tenn 2, 104, 105, 106, 223

Courtesy of the Swedish Centre for Architecture and Design 48 below, 49

UC Berkeley, Environmental Design Archives: Thomas D. Church Collection, 1933–1977 67, 76–77; Thomas D. Church Collection, 1933–1977 © Rondal Partridge Archives 69; Special Collections, University Library, UC Davis USA 73; Robert R. Royston Collection, 1941–1990 © Estate of Phil Palmer 183 above right, 183 below

AUTHOR BIOGRAPHY

Ethne Clarke is an author, editor, and horticultural consultant. She was raised in Park Forest, Illinois—a midcentury planned community—and was a student at the Kansas City Art Institute School of Design.

She is an award-winning journalist, former editor-in-chief of *Organic Gardening* and garden editor of *Traditional Home,* and a contributing editor for *House & Garden.* Ms. Clarke is internationally known as the author of a number of best-selling books on practical gardening, design and landscape history, including *Hidcote: The Making of a Garden* and *Infinity of Graces: Cecil Pinsent, an English Architect in the Italian Landscape;* her original research for these books broke new ground on their subjects.

Ms. Clarke holds a Master of Philosophy from the faculty of Fine Art, De Montfort University, England, and has lectured for garden groups and at universities around the world in her subject areas. Her research has involved a close study of architectural history between the Arts and Crafts period and early Modernism, and this has been a guiding influence on the renovation of her house and garden in Colorado—a small midcentury modern ranch built in 1958.

First published in the United Kingdom as
The Mid-Century Modern Garden by
Frances Lincoln
An imprint of The Quarto Group
The Old Brewery, 6 Blundell Street,
London N7 9BH, United Kingdom

Published in the United States of America by
Gibbs Smith
P.O. Box 667
Layton, Utah 84041
1.800.835.4993 orders
www.gibbs-smith.com

First Gibbs Smith edition 2017
21   3 2

Printed and bound in China

Library of Congress Control Number: 017932129
ISBN: 978-1-4236-4580-1

FSC
www.fsc.org

MIX
Paper from
responsible sources
FSC® C016973